GHOSTS
of Gettysburg
V

Spirits, Apparitions and Haunted Places of the Battlefield

by
Mark Nesbitt

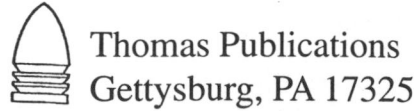

Thomas Publications
Gettysburg, PA 17325

To Katie

Yours to count on....

Sit down again together, Army of the Potomac! all that are left of us,—on the banks of the river whose name we bore, into which we have put new meaning of our own. Take strength from one more touch, ere we pass afar from the closeness of old. The old is young to-day; and the young is passed. Survivors of the fittest, it seems to us, abide in the glory where we saw them last,—take the grasp of hands, and look into the eyes, without words! Who shall tell what is past and what survives? For there are things born but lately in the years which belong to the eternities.

—Maj. Gen. Joshua Chamberlain

The shadows deepen. It has passed,—the splendid pageant; it is gone forever,—the magnificent host that streamed from the mountains to the sea; that flaming bolt which cut the Confederacy in two,—or shall we say that left its deep track upon the earth to mark the dark memories of those years; or to shine forever as a token of saving grace in the galaxy of the midnight sky?

—Maj. Gen. Joshua Chamberlain

CONTENTS

ACKNOWLEDGEMENTS

Once again, scores of individuals were helpful in putting together this work. My sincere thanks go out to those who, out of the goodness of their hearts, a love for Gettysburg and a more or less forced interest in the paranormal, have shared their strange, yet fascinating and undeniable experiences with me.

Those who related stories to me include Denise and John Ackerman, Mary Adelsberger, Jennifer Hodge and Ann Leifert, Mollie Back, Andrew Batten, Harry Borger, Corinne Brownholtz, Sara Callen, Richard Capiccioni and family, Deborah DiCaro, Duke Conover, Jim Cooke, James J. Corsetti, Jr. Esq., Suezette Dunham, John Dynia, Dr. Charles Emmons, Donald E. Evans, John Fenstermacher, the Rev. Mark Fischer, Rick Fisher, Jim Garrahy, Jason Gross, Bill Hallett, Harry I. Halloway, Aloma Handshew, Dave Hann, Michael K. Hollahan, Steve Kovall, Suzanne M. Ledger, Dianna Loski, Wendy Miller, Jennifer Moyer, Edward Newhouse, Ron Ogburn, Lorraine Ortiz, Danny and Terri Potter, Cheryl A. Raimondi, Katherine Ramsland, Betty Roche, Kerry J. Ryan, Bruce A. Sigmon, Karl Silvius, Michael Smith, Terry L. Smith, Rachel Stombaugh, Shelley Sykes, Sally Thomas, Mark C. Wilson, Sue Wilson.

Dean and Sally Thomas, and Jim Thomas all deserve thanks for this and others of my *Ghosts of Gettysburg* series. Garry Adelman, fellow author and rigid taskmaster at Thomas Publications, kept me to my task. Thanks, one and all.

I have endeavored to include everyone who contributed to this book in this list, but papers get shuffled and names get misplaced until after the book is finished. If I have not mentioned you, my sincerest apologies. Look for yourself in my next book!

INTRODUCTION

*The distinction between past, present, and future
is only an illusion, however persistent.*

—Albert Einstein

To those who say, these are good stories...if you believe in ghosts, I say: You don't have to believe in ghosts to believe these stories. All that you have to believe in are the powers of human observation, for these stories are eyewitness accounts of experiences at Gettysburg.

Still there are those who doubt what I have written and collected from the "percipients" of the paranormal at Gettysburg.

Scientists are great skeptics since paranormal experiences, they feel, cannot be recreated in a laboratory. I saw a recent TV special in which scientists had been shown photos and videos of paranormal events to watch on TVs in their labs. They proceeded to explain how easily the videos or photos could have been faked.

I am not a scientist, but I know that if you want to find out if things are faked or not, the first thing you do is watch the experiment being done. The next thing you do is try to do the experiment yourself. Not one of the scientists pronouncing the "fakes" had ever been along when the videos were being made.

I have. I have accompanied numerous "paranormal investigators" on forays into "haunted" houses, or cemeteries or battlefields. Intrigued, I purchased the equipment and have made videos and taken photos and asked questions in the silence of the darkened battlefield and have heard noises and voices recorded when there were none to be heard while recording. Nothing, I can say unequivocally, in my presence, was ever faked.

You must realize that it is obviously not the "ghosts" fault that they cannot be explained scientifically. The "ghost" is merely evidence of something that our current definition of science is too narrow to explain. Because we cannot explain why something happened or repeat it in a lab does not mean it did not happen or was not observed. Perhaps it is science that needs to change to accommodate what is going on, like it did when Newton explained through mathematics about motion and gravity, or when Einstein's theories forced science to expand even more to encompass the unseen interior world of the atom. Eminent scientific scholars once believed the universe revolved around the Earth too.

The problem with science denying the existence of "ghosts" in spite of all the collected data, is that it fails to take in the future, the potential or the possibility that one day we may have an explanation for the sightings and experiences: it

om a newly developed method or device; or perhaps from some-
fshoot—of paranormal studies, some pattern we haven't noticed
se there wasn't enough data.

I mean, if you would have told someone just fifty years ago that sand would
be doing our thinking for us in the 1980's and 90's—our calculations, our
writing, our editing, our printing—they would have considered the concept
nonsense. And yet, that is just what is forming the letters I write now—sand—
silicon—computer chips.

We're not at the end of our knowledge, so please do not sell us humans short.
About reality and what exists, we haven't yet scratched the surface.

Another group of disbelievers are the historians, especially around Gettysburg,
yet their motives are still unexplained. I consider myself an historian and admit
that our own discipline is far from scientific, history being, as one wag once
wrote, a pack of lies everyone agrees upon.

But the concise definition of history is the collection of eyewitness accounts
to an event in the past. It's as simple as that. There's no cut-off date; it can be as
recent as ten minutes ago. Strictly speaking, history doesn't even have to be
eventful—doesn't have to be the Battle of Waterloo—but can be something as
simple as diary entries, which a number of historians now publish.

The only real criterion is the veracity and the reliability of the eyewitness.

The soldiers who fought in the battle were under tremendous personal
stress: They could have been sent to their Maker at any second. So it can be
forgiven if two soldiers, fighting in the same battle within yards of one
another remembered differently the events that took place. Yet some historians are willing to take a soldier's recollections of the events on the
Gettysburg battlefield observed while under awful duress as more believable
or cogent than the recollections of a family, safe in their own automobile,
under no stress whatsoever, who happen to witness an unexplainable and
possibly paranormal event.

Finally, and perhaps the most vociferous of all doubters to the existence of
ghosts are devout religious-types who claim they are "demons" sent by the devil
to "confuse" us. Some quote scripture denying and warning about the existence
of ghosts.

And yet, in the Bible—and in other religions' primary literature—there are
found numerous references to life after death. Sixty percent of Americans
believe in a final judgement, that is, a reckoning to a higher being after one is
dead.

You who are not a scientist, or historian, or particularly religious may view
the sightings of "ghosts" with skepticism because you have never experienced
one. Subscribing to that theory, however, means that Paris never existed until I
personally visited it this past June.

But collecting close to 400 stories of peoples' paranormal experiences (and
adding to those the 300 others Dr. Charles Emmons collected in China and in
America) does two things.

First, it puts the burden on skeptics: if it were one or two sightings we've collected, well, maybe our sources are suspect. But hundreds? Could they all be mistaken as to what they witnessed on the fields of carnage?

Second, it gives us an opportunity to analyze data. Here's what we know about whatever it is that people are experiencing here at Gettysburg and other places as well:

— The subjects (aka "ghosts") may represent some sort of energy because they give off cold and sometimes heat that can be felt by persons coming in contact with them or being near them.

— The subjects reflect light and so must have some substance to them that is sometimes seen by the naked eye, but more often shows up in photographs. They may even generate their own light.

— The subjects sometimes appear white, with a bluish core and tint; other colors, particularly red, red-orange, and gold are seen. Occasionally, the entire rainbow spectrum is displayed.

— The subjects are in motion: they even rise, something cold air does not do on its own. They have been video taped moving toward, away from, and perpendicular to the camera's viewpoint.

— The subjects have electromagnetic properties. Gauss meters—electromagnetic detectors—have been seen to spike when coming in contact with the subjects. The subjects also seem to drain energy from batteries in cameras. They will activate or de-activate electronics in cameras. Perhaps it is through this electromagnetism they communicate, since magnetic tape and digital recording chips will capture sounds when there are no sounds being propagated through airwaves.

— The subjects sometimes "gather" about a human as if curious.

— The subjects sometimes move intelligently, responding to requests to move. Sometimes, it appears, they even provide answers to specific questions.

— The subjects sometimes change shape, going from "orb" shaped to a misty, ropey, cloud some refer to as "ectoplasm," to full human body (or body part) shapes.

Now, think about your own classic definition of a "ghost:" They are white and change shape; they sometimes communicate; they make the hair stand up on your body, apparently from the cold, but perhaps from electromagnetic energy; they move and seem to follow us or are at least curious about us and sometimes, for seemingly no reason, appear and disappear.

So, perhaps its time we took a closer look at what has been so vehemently denied by some, yet have been as close to us for millennia, as our own skin, our own minds, or our own souls....

MAD CARNIVAL

You may talk of gin and beer
When you're quartered safe out 'ere
An' you're sent to penny-fights an' Aldershot it;
But when it comes to slaughter
You will do your work on water,
An' you'll lick the bloomin' boots of 'im that's got it.
—Rudyard Kipling

On July 1, 1863, it was merely a meaningless, rock-strewn little hill with no name. By the next afternoon it would become an angry God's bloody anvil, roaring and flaming, with men and nations being shaped and forged and tempered upon its rocky slopes, and souls sparking off into the black abyss.

Even the soldiers did not know what it was called, this rise where they were summoned to die. Officers sometimes referred to it in their reports as "Granite Spur," or "Sugarloaf," and sometimes confused it with the larger hill just to the south. That hill eventually became known as "Round Top," probably from military necessity and perhaps coming from a colloquial name. Thus, the smaller hill became "Little Round Top." Because of the fact that it, and not its higher counterpart to the south, had been stripped of timber the autumn before, the smaller of the two became militarily significant.

By the end of the war it would be injected into the American military lexicon of elevated killing fields, like Bunker and Breed's Hills, Malvern Hill, Marye's Heights, Lookout Mountain. It remains in the common language of America, and the world, alongside other names that reverberate synonymously and imperishably with bloody courage: San Juan Hill, Pork Chop Hill, Hamburger Hill, Mount Suribachi. It echoes in the soul like other heights of glorious sacrifice: Masada, Gethsemane, Golgotha.

Military men always look for "the high ground" to defend. Tactically a hill gives the defenders a good view of the enemy. He must show you all his attacking troops while you can hide your reserves behind the hill. On Little Round Top, artillery had a clear field of fire from its summit, the only drawback being, as attacking lines got closer to the guns, they could not depress the barrels enough to hit the enemy. Yet they could still boom away, lending moral support to the infantry engaging the foe.

And even the most unsophisticated private realized that the enemy is just a man, and if he has to climb a hill before he reaches you, he'll be tired and out of breath. The chances of hitting a slow, winded target were a lot better than one running downhill at you. The enemy's chances of shooting you with a trembling rifle, or fighting effectively hand-to-hand were greatly diminished after a hard climb.

Before about 3:00 p.m. on July 2, 1863, the fate of that small hill—along with the fate of thousands of soldiers—was being decided by a handful of men.

One was Robert E. Lee, who by natural inclination and circumstances dictated by the overwhelming victory the day before, wanted to attack. He sent out scouts at dawn, and by 9:00 a.m. they were back. They had reached the summit of the smaller hill yonder and found no Yankees. Lee determined to push forward.

Another player was Major General Daniel Sickles, commander of the Federal 3rd Corps. Disappointed with the positioning of his troops in the low ground north of the two hills, he began a massive move of his entire corps westward to higher ground near a peach orchard on the Emmitsburg Road. His forward movement stretched his corps too far to cover Little Round Top and put his left flank in a jumble of boulders named by the locals, the Devil's Den just below the hill.

Another participant was Confederate General James Longstreet. After reluctantly receiving orders from Lee to have his corps attack the Federal line, he marched his troops methodically—some say too methodically—to the attack position. Because he had orders to avoid detection by signalmen now posted on the smaller of the two hills, he had to reverse his course and reroute his march, giving a certain Union engineering officer time to mount the small hill and discover a remarkable fact.

That engineer was Major General Gouverneur K. Warren, who found himself at the summit of the smaller hill along with some signalmen on the afternoon of July 2, sent there by Union Army commander Major General Meade. Longstreet had gotten his men into position, and found Sickles' Corps in advance and isolated from the rest of the Union army. Longstreet promptly attacked.

Longstreet's line overlapped Sickles' line at Devil Den, and units swept around south of the bigger hill. After climbing the precipitous south face of Big Round Top in the heat of the July afternoon, one unit, out of water when the detachment sent to fill their canteens had not returned before sudden marching orders, collapsed to a man. Five...ten minutes passed.

> *Military men call it the god of battles...they mutter it in their fervent prayers or solemn afterthoughts, after having sent thousands of men to their deaths. Others have called it fate or "fortunes of war." Military historians, try as they might with complete hindsight to explain why battles were won or lost, still come up empty-handed because the tiniest mistake that should or would have never happened did happen and altered the course of an action, a battle, a war. Some with a more mysterious bent say that it was all preordained: that the Southern Confederacy was doomed from the first*

cannon shot at Fort Sumter because this Union was meant to be indivisible. But in reality, all the military schooling in the world will not help if your men are hungry or out of water, so parched they cannot move, because orders to attack came before canteens arrived.

Meanwhile, Warren is observing Sickles' battle from the smaller of the two hills, from the great boulder which now bears his likeness in bronze. Suddenly his attention is pulled to the woods on the northwestern slope of the larger hill. He steadies his glasses but can see nothing. He sends a galloper down the hill to order a cannon in the valley to lob a shell into the wooded side of the large hill just to his south. When the shell crashes through the trees, Confederate infantrymen—in a perfectly natural reaction—flinch. The subtle movement causes burnished rifle barrels and bayonets to glint in the afternoon sun. Warren now knows that there is a large number of troops about to advance upon this undefended hill. He looks about and realizes that Confederates on this hill could be a threat to the Federal position stretching out to the north...that they could cut off retreat routes for the Union army should they capture the hill. In other words, from this small, rocky hill, the Rebels would be between the entire Union Army and the northern capitol of Washington![1]

He sends couriers to bring troops. He finally rushes down the hill himself and, through channels, gets couriers sent for some troops. Colonel Strong Vincent—movie star handsome with his high forehead, straight nose, and flaring mutton-chop sideburns so popular during the war—stops one of the couriers, wheedles the orders out of him, and rushes his own brigade—without orders—to the hill. Thus he seals his own fate.

Colonel Joshua L. Chamberlain, huge drooping moustache covering his mouth, and his two brothers, leading the 20th Maine up the slope, are almost killed by a passing shell; he sends one to the front of the line and the other to the rear. No more riding together into battle for the Chamberlain boys, for "another shot like that might make it hard on Mother."

Hazlett's Battery eventually summits the hill behind them with Warren himself leaning his major-general's gilt sword against a tree and helping to haul cannon like a common artillerist.

If not for that five or ten minutes of complete exhaustion on the top of the big hill...if not for those damned lost canteens....

The fighting is hand-to-hand in some cases. Big guns are booming from the Confederate side. Northern guns reply in a cacophony of death.

Chamberlain's and the 20th Maine's fight for the southern cusp of Little Round Top is now the stuff of legend—placed at the spot by the doomed Col. Vincent himself: "I place you here. You are to hold this ground at all hazards!" They repulsed several Confederate assaults, ran out of ammunition, and drove the Rebels off with a downhill bayonet charge that some would have you believe was a stroke of genius on the part of their commander, Chamberlain. With no disrespect meant, Chamberlain only did what any good colonel under the same orders and out of ammunition could have done: to save the high ground he had to leave it to drive the enemy away. It was a vicious fight: his antagonist, Colonel William C. Oates of the 15th Alabama recalled that, the soldiers' "blood stood in puddles in some places on the rocks."[2]

Dashing, intelligent Col. Strong Vincent, on Little Round Top via Erie, Pennsylvania, and Harvard University, has given up a law practice to join the army. In the court he is about to enter, the verdict is not always just, but the sentence is always carried out. Married to his college sweetheart, the beautiful Elizabeth Carter of Newark, he had been noticed riding gracefully with her around the camps when winter duty was light. "Their love was ideal," wrote one comrade. But he had another love, one for which he would die. Near Hanover, Pennsylvania, on the march toward Gettysburg, he orders the color guard of the 83rd Pennsylvania Volunteers to the front of the column to lead them into his home state of Pennsylvania. As the flag is unfurled and flutters by, he remarks to his adjutant in a haunting, patriotic prophecy: "What death more glorious can any man desire than to die on the soil of old Pennsylvania fighting for that flag?"

Part of Vincent's line begins to crumble, and he personally rallies it and leads them forward. A volley of fire from the advancing Confederates and the "glorious" death he had predicted was his to embrace: he falls heavily onto the rocky slope mortally wounded. Beautiful Mrs. Vincent would ride no more with her handsome, bewhiskered husband.

Brigadier General Stephen Weed's Brigade was ordered to help Sickles in his predicament, but General Warren rides down and remonstrates with Colonel Patrick O'Rorke, left in command of the brigade while Weed queried Sickles. Warren agrees to let the rest of the brigade go to Sickles if O'Rorke and his 140th New York—the largest regiment in the brigade—comes to the summit of the hill. Patrick O'Rorke, first in his class of '61 at the United States Military Academy, sees immediately the danger and detaches his regiment. His Irish luck is about to run out.

The men rush over the crest of Little Round Top and down into the faces of the Rebels without stopping to align their ranks. There is a volley and two dozen of the 140th New York topple.

Clara Bishop O'Rorke, married but a year to Patrick, becomes a widow in that instant because of an impetuous charge over the crest of that rocky little hill at Gettysburg. Her beloved Patrick, doing his duty, is made extinct by that cruel volley. Eighteen months later Clara enters a convent, to spend the rest of her life in holy devotion, for there had been only one man for her in this life.

Weed finally gets the rest of his brigade to the summit of Little Round Top, but he is shot and falls hard upon a flat rock. Hazlett, the artillerist, leans over to see about his commander and is shot dead and falls across his body.

Hundreds of other not-so-famous boys are taking the .577 caliber, soft lead minie ball deep into their bodies at 900 feet per second as well. Being hit is bad enough, with its electric-shock-like effect upon the nervous system. But upon being struck, the limbs go weak, legs buckle, and you tumble, headfirst perhaps, down upon the rocky slope. *Raise your arms to stop the fall*, the brain commands, but your arms cannot move, and on this hillside, more often than not, you will slam full-face into a sharp rock, perhaps fall on your musket, your cartridge box or haversack full of hard junk, perhaps even on your own bayonet. You will lie there then, for long minutes, or hours in the hot sun, and perhaps even days, head throbbing from the pain, body tormented by fever and chills and fear of death. Some soldiers are shot again and again, so thickly fly the minie balls in this battle for Little Round Top.

Reenactors inhabit Gettysburg often. It is fortunate that so many individuals in the "hobby" visit Gettysburg on a regular basis. They faithfully spend their Memorial Days, July Fourths, Labor Days, and Remembrance Days in Gettysburg. In recent years, the Remembrance Day parade (commemorating the November 19th anniversary of the Gettysburg Address) has had more "soldiers" and 19th century ladies in it than the original parade in 1863.

Their motive is sincere—a desire to honor the soldiers who fought here. While some question their methods—dressing up like Civil War soldiers—of honoring them, if the dead can see us like we can—occasionally—see them, they must be honored, or at least appreciative that some of us are willing to dress in the uncomfortable clothing, march in the hot sun, camp in the rain, and breathe in the sulfur smoke of battle once again.

I have only one complaint about the reenactors: they are often mistaken for ghosts!

People approach me, or write to me and tell me stories of their personal experiences on the battlefield or in the town, and of seeing in the distance a single soldier or groups of soldiers marching around or just hanging out. My first reaction is to ask the date. If the date is that of any major holiday when reenactors throng to Gettysburg, my skepticism increases.

But knowing also that on the anniversary of the battle paranormal activity increases, I must question further. If they tell me that they drove away and just left the soldier staring at them with a spooky look in his eyes, he probably went back to his campsite and shared a good laugh with his fellow reenactors about the spoof he just played upon some tourists. But if an observer sees what he or she thinks is a reenactor, and that reenactor suddenly vanishes, then obviously, something took place that does not follow the physical laws of this world as we know them.

I received two letters from a woman dated approximately eighteen months apart. Both letters recounted a visit she had in 1995 that appeared to have been an encounter with one of the spirits that continue to patrol Little Round Top.

She, her boyfriend, and his mother got to Little Round Top late. By 9:00 p.m. in August the sun has pretty much disappeared from the western sky. From

Little Round Top, the horizon above the South Mountain range mixes dusky hues: blue, a hint of green, a deep red the color of dried blood. As the visitors leave, group by group, the hill takes on an almost magical, unworldly aura.

The boyfriend strolled to the left, toward the castle-shaped monument to the 44th New York Infantry; his mother went to the right; our subject who was about to catch a glimpse into the past, stood near the edge of the northern end of Little Round Top. She was standing at about the spot where the bold Col. Vincent rode ahead of his troops, with his eye for terrain seeking the perfect place to establish a defensive line, and later where Col. Chamberlain rode past to place his men where Vincent commanded.

She looked off in the distance at the great boulders of Devil's Den. In the darkness of the battlefield, the mind sometimes plays tricks. But she was absolutely certain of the feeling she got—behind her back, she was sure, something was staring at her.

She turned around and there, sitting astride a large horse, glaring straight at her, was a soldier. She recalled that he was dressed in a blue uniform, with a large-brimmed hat and tall boots. She knew it was a uniform, for on the breast were two parallel rows of shiny buttons. "I remember the buttons gleamed very brightly," she wrote.

At first she thought the man might be a park ranger, so she turned and called to her boyfriend. She remembered calling out and then immediately feeling terrified. She turned back, wondering perhaps if the horseman was approaching her in the darkness behind her back. But the horseman was gone, disappearing in the instant it took to turn her head one way, then the other. While she remembered the boots, the hat, the blue uniform and specifically the double rows of bright buttons, she never got to see his face, nor could she remember anything about it. It was almost as if he had no face.

There are several things to analyze here. First of all, park rangers wear green pants and gray shirts; second, the Park Service has not had horse patrols since the mid-1970s; third, it was August 20, no date of any significance for reenactors to be at Gettysburg; fourth, she sent a picture, and the site she indicated where the horseman appeared is in the open, with no large clump of trees for a horse and rider—no small mass—to hide behind quickly; fifth, the uniform she described, especially the button pattern, matches the double-breasted frock coat prescribed for colonels in the army manual....

"This man has haunted me for years,"she wrote. "It's just like he came home with me in my mind.... I wish I could see him again just so I know what his face looked like."

Imagine that her wish came true, and somehow, completely out of reason, she had the opportunity to see him again, and gaze into that face she missed seeing before. Would she see a handsome, sophisticated face, with thick mutton-chop sideburns, or one with deepset eyes and a huge moustache, flowing over his mouth, soldiers once, visitors again, and again, returning to the site where they met fate face-to-face?

A young reenactor from Brewer, Maine, birthplace of Joshua L. Chamberlain, recounted in a letter his experience on the back slope of Little Round Top while he was here to participate in the filming of the movie *Gettysburg*. Like so many reenactors who were extras for the film and who camped *en masse* just beyond the Eisenhower Farm in the rear of Longstreet lines, he casually mentioned that he and the others had "many experiences with ghosts," while here. But one in particular stood out in his mind.

One evening, he and a friend visited the monument to the 20th Maine. Perhaps he knew of men from his home town who had fought upon that ground: Private A. W. Fickett, an 18-year-old farmer, or John T. Given, a clerk in one of the stores in Brewer. Maybe he had done enough research to recall other names from a dusty roster. There was machinist Frank Burr, also a private, and 22 year old Charles N. Ayer.[3] All were prepared to give up their lives and their futures in Maine for something, as their commander, Joshua Chamberlain would later say, "of gravest import for ourselves, for others, for our Country, for man everywhere."

After paying their respects the reenactors decided to try and find the monument to Co. B, 20th Maine, detached by Chamberlain to watch the left flank and thought by him at one time during the battle to be lost, killed, or captured. The reenactor wanted to place a flag at the monument, in sincere respect, since that was the reenactment company to which he belonged.

The trail to the marker for Co. B is now well used; then, before the movie made the 20th Maine the most popular regiment in the Civil War, the site was obscure. He and his friend found the horse trail that meanders behind Little Round Top, and got to a huge pine tree, but could not find the monument. But standing at the tree—possibly one that had witnessed the battle—in the growing darkness, he said they both began to get a "very cold and strange feeling. The hair on the back of our necks stood up on end." They decided their direction was wrong, and so they turned back, intending to return to the rest of their unit.

Not ready yet to abandon his mission to lay the flag at the monument, the young man decided to go back by himself. Retracing his steps in the advancing dusk, he passed through the area where, as they continued to stretch their line to the right, the Confederates of William C. Oates' 15th Alabama trod. Unless he had read Oates' account of *The War Between the Union and Confederacy* he might not have known of the hardships the Confederates had suffered on that very ground he passed over.

Oates described the advance of his line into the musketry of the Maine men as wavering, "like a man trying to walk against a strong wind." Oates saw his own brother, John, riddled by Yankee lead, falling mortally wounded. Before the battle, John had been behind the lines, ill, and William had advised him to stay out of the next fight. He refused, stating prophetically that he did not want to be called a coward or disgrace the uniform he wore: "I shall go through, unless I am killed, which I think is very likely."

Somewhere near where the reenactor walked, Oates saw a man named Keils from Henry County, Alabama run past him, his throat cut open by a bullet, spraying blood over everyone he ran past at every labored breath. Oates stood next to Capt. J. Henry Ellison, the son of a Methodist minister, to whom he had given a fine new uniform upon his promotion. Ellison had approached Oates to hear an order, turned to shout the command to his men, and was shot through the head. "I saw the ball strike him," recalled Oates. "That is, I was looking at him when it did. He fell upon his left shoulder, turned upon his back, raised his arms, clenched his fists, gave one shudder, his arms fell, and he was dead."[4]

The reenactor found himself back at the ancient tree they had visited a few minutes before, and leaned back against the tree to rest and get his bearings. As he looked off to the left through the gathering darkness, he saw a person standing just a few feet away. But this was no ordinary visitor to the remote, scarcely-visited area. He, apparently at one time, had been there before.

The reenactor described him as wearing a butternut colored shell jacket—the color Confederates dyed their homespun, short jackets trying to make them gray—and sky-blue trousers—which many Confederates wore at Gettysburg, having stripped the dead Yankees after their recent victory at Chancellorsville. He carried a carpet bag haversack—typical of that period in the war—and wore a slouch hat—the nondescript, floppy hat loved by the Southerners for its utility as a sunshade, water-carrier, and pillow.

Whoever this totally authentic Confederate was, he had not seen the reenactor yet. He pulled out a pipe, stuffed some tobacco in it and lit it, wreaths of pungent smoke making their way over to the young man from Brewer, who by now could smell it.

Figuring it was a fellow reenactor of the Confederate persuasion, come to see one of the more remote areas of the field, he called out a cheery, "Hello." "He looked at me," he wrote, "with a face of surprise and vanished." Taken by surprise by the living, he apparently returned to the dead.

In May 1997, a group of friends from a nearby college came to Gettysburg for some relaxation between the end of classes and finals. They spent some time lounging on the rocks at Devil's Den, and taking in the general beauty that permeates the battlefield during the spring. It was evening, approaching dusk. They knew of the ghost stories associated with the area, but had nothing out of the ordinary occur. They assumed it would be an uneventful visit.

It was about 9:30 p.m., and they realized that they would have to leave the battlefield soon. They decided to visit Little Round Top one last time before they went back to school, then off to their hometowns for the summer.

By the time they reached the summit, they were alone. The sun had set, and in the darkness they had some quiet time to ponder the feats accomplished where they stood now. They thought of young men about their age, breasting sheets of flame and wreathed by smoke, watching good friends fall and be swallowed by the smoke and rugged slope.

Gradually they made their way to the cannon of Hazlett's Battery that once shouted hoarse defiance with fire over the heads of comrades. All was quiet now. Thoughts of seeing anything supernatural had been erased from their minds by the reverie of a lovely spring night. Then, as they stood to the muzzles of the guns, like their youthful counterparts thirteen decades before, it came to them, each and every one: the acrid, foul-smelling, rotten-egg odor of burnt black powder, like sulfur and charcoal, stinging their nostrils. Individual confusion gave way to group recognition of what they were smelling out of time and logic. Then mass panic took over, and they bolted for their cars, taking home with them to their summer vacations a little reminder of just one of the sensory experiences the Battle of Gettysburg had been...and continues to be.

In 1992 a woman and her family were traveling from the East Coast to relocate in the West and decided to stop in Gettysburg for her first visit here. Her husband, however, had been a Civil War buff and had visited a number of times. She admits to possessing ESP, but she, like all those with the "gift" merely accepted it. Yet the experience she had at Gettysburg continued to haunt her for six years, until she felt compelled to write.

They only had a few hours for their visit in October, and it was already late in the day. They had gotten to Little Round Top at dusk. He, of course, had already seen the hill numerous times where so many had spilled out their life's blood in defense of a future for the states united as one country, so he stayed in the car with their infant son.

She decided, with the sun on the wane, to take a quick look around, take as many photos as she could to study later, and return to the car. She was in a hurry, her mind on many different things at once, distracted, and not realizing that it was whenever she was in that state of distraction that she had always been more susceptible to the reception of subtle vibrations from the other world.

On her way up she kept "seeing" something on the rocks in her peripheral vision—out of the corner of her eye. When she looked directly at it, it would disappear, but in her side vision it was all too clear, and all too vivid. What she saw was fresh blood, lying in pools upon the dusky rocks. Each time she snapped her head to focus on one crimson pool, it would evaporate before her eyes.

She got to the summit, took her pictures, and with just a little apprehension of what else she might see, began her trip down to the car. She never saw the apparitional blood again.

Since she was familiar with her "gift," and was unfamiliar with the history of Little Round Top, she attributed no significance to the event. It was not until she was watching Ken Burns' documentary *The Civil War* that it hit her.

She and her husband were watching the segment on Gettysburg in the comfort of her TV room. Her mind was relaxed, taking in the Civil War images and haunting music of the classic series. Suddenly, her experience at Gettysburg the previous year turned her mind topsy-turvy. An officer was being quoted about his fight on Little Round Top: "the blood stood in puddles on some of the rocks." According to her, every hair on her body stood on end, and it was like she had the wind knocked out of her.

She wrote that, even though she had psychic experiences before, she "never expected to have such a powerful, spiritual knockout punch from one of them. To date, I still have this unnatural urge to return there so that my questions may be answered. But where do I find answers when I don't even know what the questions are?"

In a place like Gettysburg, where there was so much mayhem concentrated in one relatively small area, death almost takes on a viable persona. Not death, but Death. And while we, from this side, look at Death as the great mystery, those on the other side are as familiar with him (or her) as we are with life. But we, stranded temporarily on this side, must remember that Death not only presents us with innumerable questions, it also, eventually, answers them all.

The view toward Devil's Den from the summit of Little Round Top.

DYING GAME

Soldiers are citizens of Death's gray land.
—Siegfried Sassoon

Some 180 million years ago a diabase sill intruded through the floor of Triassic Age sandstone and shale that had been laid down in a basin 25 miles wide and over 100 miles long. These intrusions of what geologists call sills and dikes in the late Triassic would form hills and ridges which would be named by the settlers of the area, most of whom, since geology was an infant science then, could not care less about what lay more than plow's depth beneath their feet.

Geologists would study the area and name the broad plain the Gettysburg Basin after the most famous town encompassed by it. What they call a diabase dike, upon which a religious school would be moved, was named by the locals Seminary Ridge. An outcrop of what geologists would name the Gettysburg Sill would become Cemetery Ridge to military men and historians. South of the town, a jumble of massive rocks and boulders would one day be identified by geologists as diabase—a combination of crystalline silicates of sodium, calcium and aluminum—but was always known to the locals as the Devil's Den.[1]

If all this seems rather pedantic for a "ghost book," it is not. The lay of the land dictates tactics from the highest-ranking general officer down to the individual soldier's level; it always has—and it always will. And the type of crystalline rock outcroppings may offer one clue to why there have been so many residual hauntings, noises out of time, and visions of the past.

While Army commanders like Robert E. Lee and George Gordon Meade looked at the area around Gettysburg for hills upon which to anchor flanks and ridges from which to launch or repel attacks, corps commanders looked for good, level roads to move large numbers of troops, artillery and supply wagons quickly and upon which to retreat in case of trouble or to move wounded to the rear. Brigade and regimental commanders sought hills with rock walls or good soil, to dig into and build breastworks for their men to hide behind.

The men? All they wanted was a swale in the ground about eyeball level, behind which they could stand (which you had to do to load the rifle musket), be hidden from the enemy, and pick him off as he crested the ridge in front. Sunken roads were often the perfect depth, which is why there is mention of so many of them in Civil War histories. Later, of course, as breechloading bolt and semiautomatic weapons became the common soldier's armament, all they needed was a depression of about a foot or two: just enough cover to lie behind.

It is called "defilade," and to the footsoldier bearing the brunt of every battle, it is sweet life itself. Many a loving mother's son came home from the most horrible of battles because his drill sergeant taught him to see defilade in an apparently flat field, and to go to it and use it. That is why even the smallest changes in a historic site—the building of a new road, or laying of sewer pipe, let alone the construction of a new center for the visitor—are abhorrent to the true historian. Every swale at Gettysburg may have saved someone's precious life.

In other words, geologists and locals may have named the hills, valleys, and rock outcroppings around the little Pennsylvania town of Gettysburg, but it was the soldiers who fought and died here who sanctified it with their blood.

The huge boulders of Devil's Den and the adjoining field at the top of the Den, shaped in the geometric form of a triangle, were a hurricane of combat for just a few short hours of American history. Between 4:00 p.m. and 7:00 p.m., on July 2, 1863, Hood's Division of Lt. Gen. James Longstreet's Corps did what he later would call, the "best three hours' fighting ever done by any troops on any battlefield."

It may have been good fighting, but it was also costly. It began with a huge bombardment by Longstreet's artillery. Union soldiers in the area tried in vain to burrow into the stone-solid ground and had to settle for finding rocks to hide behind. Artillery did not leave much after it struck a man or exploded nearby. One shell that afternoon blew apart as many as fifteen men at a time; others were decapitated or sliced in half, throwing brains and entrails across the survivors.[2] Union artillery, meantime, took out Major General J. B. Hood with a wound to the left arm.

The "diabase intrusions" took their toll as well: the Confederate advance was slowed and exhausted by some of the most difficult terrain they had encountered. As the 1st Texas approached the Triangular Field, some heard the deadly iron canister from Smith's Union Battery ring ominously off the rocks, something they knew canister did not do when it hit human flesh and bone. As the Texans advanced up the field, they were met by the men of the 124th New York, the "Orange Blossoms," from Orange County in southern New York. Texas and New York in that same small triangular field produced, what Garry Adelman and Timothy Smith vividly describe in *Devil's Den: A History and Guide*, as "a virtual carpet of blue, gray and red."

Fighting in the peculiar Triangular Field was particularly vicious, with Southern attacks like waves at the seashore, rolling up the hill then being pushed back down again by obstinate Northerners. They fought over the still warm bodies of comrades scythed down by shell, canister, and minie ball. James Cromwell, the 22-year-old Union major of the 124th New York, badgered his commander Colonel Ellis to let him charge the disorganized Texans. Ellis relented, and the decision cost both men their lives in the weirdly-shaped field.

Later, "Rock" Benning's Georgia regiments would launch at least four assaults up through the field. Some of the troops being torn up by Smith's Battery and the infantry on the crest were the men of the 15th Georgia.

According to the report of their Colonel D. M. DuBose, they took into the Triangular Field between 330 and 335 men. They walked out with less than half. Not only were the men cut to pieces, but so were whole families, left back in Georgia to ponder for years what horrible deaths their sons and brothers and sweethearts and husbands had suffered in some Pennsylvania farm field.[3]

Devil's Den and the Triangular Field have gained a reputation over the years as sites where cameras, for some bizarre, possibly paranormal, definitely unexplainable reason, refuse to work. That is not necessarily the case.

Many cameras do work just fine in both places. I, and others, have taken hundreds of photos in the Triangular Field and Devil's Den that have developed into good images of the subject matter that was framed in the view finder.

But then there was the time when three cameras all jammed at once...and the television crew that had to give up because their $13,000 camera went haywire...and the crew that came to film a reenactment of that event had their camera go completely berserk trying to film the other crew whose three battery packs went dead one-by-one as they stood in the Triangular Field....

Some people have taken it upon themselves to experiment in the Triangular Field. Dale Kaczmarek of the prestigious Ghost Research Society and I did a sweep of the field with all his scientific equipment and found that the field was as normal as your back yard.

I received through my publisher an e-mail from a serious photographer who spent three days shooting pictures in the Triangular Field after reading *Ghosts of Gettysburg*. He used four different cameras, all top of the line, and several types of film including high speed infrared, color infrared, and photo micrography film. He took over 1,000 photos over the three days.

Since he knew the Triangular Field was eventually won over by the Confederates, he wore a Federal kepi, and sang patriotic Union songs. He varied his exposure times from long to 1/4000 of a second, and moved the camera position to nine different sites.

At no time did his equipment malfunction and the film all came out of developing with nothing strange, weird, paranormal or otherworldly upon it. He has taken photos at other historic sites, both here—including the Cashtown Inn—and overseas with no anomalies. He also admitted that, while he is a skeptic, no one would have been happier than he if he had gotten something out of the ordinary, so he was also receptive to the possibility of a spiritual encounter. But that does not explain why I still get dozens of letters from people who, for no known reason, have problems with cameras in the area.

There was the lady with a Canon AE-1 camera. She had used it for 12 years without a single failure and had it completely cleaned and reconditioned specifically for her trip to Gettysburg. She had finished her roll of 36 exposures at Devil's Den and went to The Angle, the spot where the forlorn hope of forlorn hopes—Pickett's Charge—had crashed itself in a bloody tide against the Federal Second Corps. There she tried to rewind the film. It jammed and the rewind arm unscrewed in her hand. She replaced the arm, worrying about having to take the camera to a repair store to extract the film. Walking toward the Visitor Center she tried one more time to rewind the film. It suddenly began to work again.

When the roll was developed, in one of the photos, there is a shadow—without a body accompanying it—of a kneeling soldier, taking aim over the top of a rock, a photographic reminder that the men whose sacrifice made this ground hallowed are never very far away from us.

I received a letter from an aerospace engineer, a person whose profession working with the Space Shuttle demands clear, logical, analytical thinking. Yet he was confused about something that happened to his camera in 1995 while exploring the Triangular Field. He had not read any of the *Ghosts of Gettysburg* book series and so was not familiar with any of the documentation of camera failures in that three-sided killing ground. While his father waited at the top of the field, he descended the slope, then began working his way back up, taking pictures along the right hand side of the field.

He was using a modern 35 mm Single Lens Reflex camera, one he had used for years taking shots of the battlefield. He reached the end of the roll and sat on a rock to reload. As he began to rewind, the camera jammed for the first time ever in all his experience with it. He tried to unjam it for a few seconds, then decided he would have to sacrifice the first few pictures on the roll to open the back of the camera. As he did so, he was amazed to find that about 3/4 of an inch of film was jammed into the springs of the pressure plate that holds the film flat against the shutter. His analytical mind kicked in: the way the film was jammed should have been impossible since when loading film, the camera's uptake sprockets turn the film in the opposite direction. Yet the film was jammed so tightly that he could hold the camera up by the film. He was nonplussed about how the film could have done anything so unnatural...until he picked up *Ghosts of Gettysburg* and learned of the unexplained effects the field has upon image-recording equipment.

As we know from the experiences of at least two professional television film crews, still cameras are not the only cameras affected by the unknown and unexplainable at the Triangular Field.

A history teacher from Tennessee and his wife were in Gettysburg one Memorial Day weekend, took one of our *Ghosts of Gettysburg Candlelight Walking Tours*R and decided to visit the infamous Triangular Field the next day. It was a rainy Sunday, but he wanted to get some pictures of the strange field before they left. Parking the car, they walked over to the field. He passed through the gate and into the field and his wife began to "pan" the field with their video camera, going from left to right.

They returned home and viewed the tape. Her photography was excellent. She had panned the field, beginning from the left, where once the guns of

Smith's Battery trimmed the scrub brush—and mowed down brave Sons of the South—with their canister. As her camera moved to the right, it filmed her husband, and also the site where Benning's Georgians received the iron and lead compliments of Smith's boys and the 124th New York. Continuing to the right, she got a fine picture of her husband, and began to film the site where young men following the Lone Star flag took such devastating fire from the New Yorkers who stood about where she stood now, though under much more dire circumstances. Then, although she had continued filming into the woods, there, at the wall, the tape had simply stopped recording, as if someone were saying, *this time we will let you film our famous field, the one we fought and died in, but you may record nothing beyond it....*

In the spring of 1994 a Pennsylvania man invited to Gettysburg two friends with whom to share his enthusiasm for the battlefield. For the special occasion he borrowed his mother's camcorder, a Panasonic Omnivision, and supplied a high quality videotape. They rented a tape tour of the battlefield, but the man had supplemented the tape with some photo books that he had brought. So that he could manipulate the books, his friend took over the taping.

About 8:00 p.m., his two friends left and he decided to take a quick look at the video they had just shot. It was a quick review of the tour they just finished. At Devil's Den, he had told them of the trouble with cameras in the Triangular Field, documented in my books. Watching the video, he hears himself tell his friends of the famous photo of the Confederate "sharpshooter" behind the barricade in Devil's Den and how the poor soul was actually dragged there and posed by photographers just to get a good shot. He showed them the photo in the book, and on tape he can hear his friend comment on the ghoulish acts of the photographers by saying, "That was dumb." Within seconds, lines begin to cross the image on the tape. They become wide bars of snow and interference, and the audio portion becomes muffled. The interference lasts about 15 seconds. Then the image for the rest of the tape, just like the image in the beginning of the tape before he mentioned the young "sharpshooter," was fine.

Cameras are not the only things that occasionally fail to work in that area. One of the guides for the *Ghosts of Gettysburg Candlelight Walking Tours®* told me of a young woman from a local college who, after one of his tours, told him how, when she was in the Triangular Field, her wristwatch ceased to work. When he told me this, I was interested in the fact that, of all the places for a watch to stop, it happened in the field in which so many other modern devices are affected. Yet, while time continues to chip away, second by tedious second, at our lives, all watches must stop eventually. Odd coincidence that hers stopped in that field where so many young men's lives were stopped....

I thought it a coincidence until I received a letter from a former employee of mine who went on to work as a National Park Ranger and serves, in his spare time, as a Boy Scout leader as well as a reenactor. In 1998 he returned to Gettysburg with some scouts for some weekend camping.

After dinner, he read from my books until the scouts demanded a "ghost walk" on the battlefield. His reenactment unit is the 124th New York and so he decided to take them to the Triangular Field. Along the way, driving through the darkened battlefields, he told of the strange occurrences and camera failures which happened to those caught within the energy lines of the three-sided field.

One of the scouts was an avowed skeptic. He wanted to test the spirits in the Triangular Field. Let them, if they dare, interfere with his "Indiglo" watch. He pressed the button to light up the face in the darkness. Yes, everyone saw it— the watch was working fine. He brazenly strode into the field.

He got about fifteen feet down the slope and...nothing happened. Appearing very smug at his victory over the spirits of the Civil War soldiers, he turned and began to make his way out of the field, escorted by two older, female Explorer Scouts. He stopped one more time, at the gate, to check his watch. Suddenly he and the two girls rushed to the leader's side.

"My watch doesn't work anymore," he said, showing the face to the leader. "It was illuminated," wrote the leader, "but the display was wildly flashing random numbers and symbols. He was goggle-eyed and white as a ghost. His father, who had been nearby the whole time, swore to me that the boy had done nothing to sabotage his watch, and had been in his sight the whole time. One of the girls also told me that, just when the watch began to run amok, she felt as if she was suddenly hemmed in on all sides by invisible bodies. Needless to say, we left the field at once, and did not return until the following day (in broad daylight). To my knowledge, the watch still refuses to function properly."

A woman wrote to me in 1997. She, her husband and her 18-year-old son had taken a rival ghost tour and the young man had been fascinated by what the guide had said about Devil's Den. It was already 9:30 p.m., but he wanted to go out to the dark fields of desolation immediately.

The woman and her husband thought our competition's tour was "cute," but that there was probably little or no truth to the "ghost stories" they told. Her son was insistent, however, about seeing the battlefield at night, so to prove to him that all these stories about spooks were just myths and local folklore, they agreed to go.

Some have theorized that the entities can actually see us from the other side. Why else would there have been so many sightings at the extras' campsite for the filming of the movie Gettysburg? *Or why do reenactors, dressed in uniforms and hooped dresses familiar to the souls long gone to the "other plane," seem to have more paranormal experiences at Gettysburg than those of us dressed in modern civilian clothing? One can only speculate....*

They arrived at the parking area. It was extremely dark so the mother pulled out a brand new Maglite, 5-D cell flashlight they had purchased just before coming to Gettysburg. They had used it for about fifteen minutes before they got to Devil's Den. With the attitude that she just wanted to get this little side trip over with so they could go back to their cabin, the woman hopped out of the truck. The flashlight died. At first, although the batteries were new, she thought that, for some reason, they had failed. So she found a pack of brand new batteries in the truck, loaded them and...the flashlight still would not work.

The son was insistent, so they decided to just take a walk up the road, staying to the road since now they had no light. She instructed her son to walk in front of them so that he would not get lost.

It was an extremely dark night and she almost immediately lost sight of her son. Suddenly she heard someone run up behind her, breathing heavily. Thinking it was her son who had circled around them, she turned and said, "I thought I told you to stay in front."

"I am in front of you," came the reply from her son who, within a few seconds was standing in front of her. Her husband walked around to where the noise had come from but found no one there.

They continued up the road and approached the first big bend. Her son froze. She was shocked to hear him say, "I'm not going any farther; there's something bad up there." They decided to return to the truck and leave.

They backed out of the Devil's Den parking area and began taking the quickest way out—up the steep government avenue toward the Taneytown Road. But just before they began ascending the south slope of Little Round Top, her husband and son decided they wanted to take a little walk in a field to their left. It was only later she found out the name of the field: The Valley of Death.

The men got out but she remained with the truck. They were gone three...four...five minutes. Without her flashlight, she was getting a little edgy.

The battlefield is a forlorn, forsaken place at night anyway...not knowing about what happened right where you are located is the best defense against that sudden clutching at your gut, the night chills, the hair on the back of your neck going wild. But you do not have to be a historian to assume that, exactly where you are sitting or standing, some poor young man, after having suffered the ever-increasing fear of his own sudden death in battle, then to actually be struck by the wicked soft bullet or piece of iron shell, would begin to see and feel death's rapacious hunger. Perhaps on the spot you occupy, some boy's spirit left his mortal form and began its incredible journey to....

Then she heard it. Footsteps on the road ahead of her. Not one person, not five, but a dozen or more, all coming directly for the truck. She was concerned about a large number of people she could not see approaching her in the dark, alone, in the truck, in the middle of one of the greatest fields of death and destruction in the world. They kept coming closer and closer to the truck. The group seemed very large indeed, and in that total darkness, it seemed like a whole company of men. But nothing frightened her like what happened next.

She pulled on the truck headlights, and they illuminated...nothing. And with the light, the heavy clomping of a score or more feet died into silence.

Terrified, she called out into the darkness for her husband and son to return to the truck. She waited. Would they ever return? Suddenly, they were at her door. They climbed in the truck and were gone from the Valley of Death. Though they returned the next day in the bright, cheery daylight to Devil's Den, she adamantly refused to leave the truck.

They had their pictures developed of the Valley of Death; some who have seen them say that against one of the trees is the image of the face of a soldier. Indeed, inspection under a magnifying glass shows the trunk of the tree distorted, out of focus. Discernable in that spot seems to be the broad countenance of a man with a wide, full moustache, and drooping, sad eyes.

One more thing: a P.S. to her letter. When they got back to the cabin that night, their flashlight...of course, you guessed it. It worked fine and has worked ever since.

A man from Michigan had some bizarre occurrences in 1994 and 1995. One of them indicates that the paranormal power of Gettysburg reaches far beyond the surveyor's marked boundaries on this earth.

He had gone to the Triangular Field with his video camcorder. He had just purchased a fresh, brand-new battery for the device and had it fully charged. At the moment he began filming the Triangular Field, he lost total power, much like the professional camera crew had with their three battery packs. "This has never happened before or since," he wrote.

Replaying his tape of Gettysburg for the first time a week after he returned home, he was startled by what he heard recorded on the tape as he filmed the monument to the Irish Brigade. In a voice his friends attest is not his, there are three distinct, human moans recorded on the tape. He is certain he did not hear the awful echoes of the aftermath of battle when he was recording—*that* he would have remembered.

And finally, to all those who wish to take a memento from this hallowed ground home with them—a warning: It is not only against Federal law to remove anything from a battlefield, but it is also, apparently, against another, higher, unwritten law, from an unseen government.

The man was near the monument to the 20th Maine on Little Round Top. Not realizing that it was forbidden to remove anything from the battlefield, he picked up a small stone to put in his collection at home. "While that stone was in my possession," he wrote, "my world turned upside down."

Three separate times within a month of his return from Gettysburg he came home to find his kitchen wastebasket sitting in the middle of his bed in his bedroom. For a week, then, nothing happened. One night, coming home from work, there it was again: the kitchen wastebasket up on his bed. As well, a prized signed and numbered print was hanging on the wall...upside down. The print is of the most famous Confederate general officers—Lee, Jackson, Longstreet, Stuart—and their staffs at Fredericksburg, Virginia in December 1862—the same

Battle of Fredericksburg where Joshua L. Chamberlain and the men of the 20th Maine lay through the freezing day and night behind the dead bodies of the brave men who assaulted Marye's Heights before them. Some of those very men who used their comrades' corpses to shield them from bullets would be corpses themselves on the little hill at Gettysburg where the man found his souvenir rock.

Looking around the room, the man noticed one thing. The stone from the portion of Little Round Top that the 20th Maine saved at the cost of their lives...was gone.

In 1999, a man wrote to me to tell me about his family's trip to Gettysburg. They were familiar with my books and, upon reading my most recent one, their 15-year-old son was really interested in returning to Gettysburg, and taking his camera out to Devil's Den to get some pictures of the "ghosts" around the area. His father laughed, but promised they would go to Gettysburg.

The father admitted that he "somewhat" believes in ghosts, but, of course, as fathers will, he began to tease his son on the ride to Gettysburg about photographing the spirits that may remain around Devil's Den.

It was a beautiful July day when they toured the battlefield. They finally arrived at Devil's Den and began exploring the great boulders which first hid live soldiers during the battle, and corpses for years after the battle. The whole time the father was good-naturedly joking with his son about the ghosts. He, his wife, and son were walking along the tops of some of the larger rocks. He went to lift his leg to take a small step onto another rock, but, for some unknown reason, his foot remained aloft and he tumbled forward, landing on his hands and knees and losing his hat on the ground. "It seemed," he wrote, "as if something, or somebody, held my foot in place while my momentum carried me forward and downward." This he realized later. At the moment he only felt embarrassment at his apparent clumsiness.

Not hurt, he continued walking around the Den with his family. Again, he began his "all-in-good-fun" taunting of his son and his mission to photograph ghosts. They came to a fence. Still laughing and taunting, he lifted his leg to go over the fence. As he put it, "some force held my leg in place and I tumbled over." Again unhurt, he brushed himself off and told his son that his ghosts were haunting him now and attempting to deliver a message. His son was probably a little worried about his father when he, in seeming disregard for his own safety, began his teasing again.

Ten minutes later he tripped and nearly fell to the ground again. That was it. Enough is enough. Remembering from childhood, his grandmother's admonition that if something happens three times there is a message behind it, he ceased teasing his son and began recording pictures with his digital camera. The rest of their battlefield visit was uneventful.

When the family got back home, the father decided to download some of his pictures. The man is a skeptic. He wrote that he was aware that if people look hard enough at a photo, they just might see what they are looking for, and that the imagination can run wild and find images that are not really there. With all that in mind, as the first photos of his visit to Devil's Den began to slowly download onto his computer screen, they began to show the undeniable.

The first photo shows what looks like the shadowy figure of a man wearing a slouch hat (as Confederates often did), sitting in a tree (as sharpshooters often did). The second picture he calls "truly amazing." There are five or six faces visible in the image.

But his interpretation of his experiences of being tripped up by some unseen force may have taken on a more frightening, and perhaps even sinister nature, if he had read a letter I have had in my files since 1995.

A woman who had grown up in Hunterstown—just north of Gettysburg and the site of a cavalry battle of its own—wrote to me and told me of an experience that she and a girlfriend had in June 1980. In her words, "A friend of mine and I ran into your Confederate soldier in Devil's Den...."

It was night. They knew they were not supposed to be on the battlefield after 10:00 p.m., but that, of course, to local teenagers, makes it all the more fun. They had been cavorting on the rocks, leaping from one to another, when the young woman lost her footing and fell, sliding partway down into one of the many fissures in the huge boulders.

Her friend ran over and grabbed her hand to help her out, but she had this feeling...something seemed to be tugging on her foot.

She looked down. There, in the cleft of the rock, stained, exhausted, ragged, hanging on to her ankle was a Confederate soldier. She screamed, but got enough of a look at him to see that he appeared to want to get out of there, too. Her girlfriend peered into the darkness and saw the tattered arm and hand attached to the Rebel soldier holding her friend. She, too, screamed, dropped her friend and ran. Fear can be a powerful motivator. Somehow the young woman broke loose—or perhaps the real nature of the soldier that held her allowed her ankle to slip through his wispy fingers—and followed her girlfriend out of Devil's Den.

Sadly, a month later her friend passed away.

In the early 1990s, the woman was thumbing through a book on the Civil War and came upon the famous photograph of the dead Rebel soldier who was posed by photographers. She had to put the book down...the face on the dead soldier looked all too familiar.

Much has been said about the "cold spots" historically associated with ghosts. Dr. Charles Emmons has noted that it is important that people feel the temperature change *before* they have the paranormal experience, so it is not a physiological "fright" reaction to what they are experiencing. But I have spoken to numerous others who have experienced a rise in temperature as well.

In 1992, I received a letter from a reenactor from New Jersey who had some strange experiences around the time of the anniversary of Abraham Lincoln's Gettysburg Address. Like many reenactors, he had always felt a strong "presence from the other side," whenever he visited Gettysburg. He and two friends went out onto the battlefield dressed in their Civil War replica coats and forage caps. They wanted to find the spot where the poor Confederate was dragged to pose for a death study. It was a cold evening, about 5:00 p.m. when they found it. He estimated the temperature at about 30 degrees as they exited the car, but as they approached the famous spot, a strange thing occurred. The closer they got to the stone barricade, the warmer the temperature got until it was actually hot.

Admittedly, rocks will hold heat from the hot afternoon sun in the summertime. But if the temperature was already below freezing at 5:00 p.m., it had probably been a pretty cold day to begin with. Still, thinking that perhaps the sun had warmed the rocks, they shrugged off the gross temperature change and moved on.

They arrived at the monument for the 7th New Jersey, the unit they portray as reenactors. One of the three was dressed as a Confederate. While standing at the monument, the writer of the letter began telling the Confederate reenactor of the role the unit played in the battle, of the courage and sacrifice of the men from New Jersey, fighting for Pennsylvania and the Union. As they stood at the monument, the "enemy" soldier began to address Colonel Louis Francine, the commander of the 7th who was mortally wounded near the spot: "Well, Colonel, I think your boys did a real good job here..." He had hardly finished the sentiment when, from across the cold fields of death came a warm breeze which passed through the men, swirled around the monument, passed through them again and was gone.

The men went into Gettysburg for dinner, then a drink at a local tavern right across from the National Cemetery, looking for some fellow reenactors. When they found none, they decided to take a walk through the cemetery.

The author of the letter was familiar with some of the men buried there and their stories.

Perhaps he told the story of Captain William Miller, 3rd Pennsylvania Cavalry, who won the Medal of Honor for disobeying an order while fighting J. E. B. Stuart's Confederate cavalry three miles east of Gettysburg. It took three decades for him to finally get his medal, however, from a stingy Congress, and so he only had a few years to enjoy it. Perhaps he told the story of the statue of Maj. Gen. John Reynolds, whose memorial was made a more fitting tribute to the warrior by using melted down cannon barrels supplied by his native state, Pennsylvania, for his bronze figure. Or perhaps he told of Private George Nixon, 73rd Ohio Infantry, to whom the call of patriotism was so strong that, at the age of 40, he left his wife and nine children to assure that this country would "not perish from the earth," was mortally wounded on July 3, 1863, and lies buried here. His sacrifice, in some way, allowed his great-grandson, Richard, to become president of the United States.

Their tour of the cemetery was enhanced by some unseen "guides." Each time he mentioned a name, his little group would walk through what he termed "a plane" of warm air, not once, but several times. "Might it have been the soldiers," he asked, "answering the call of their names?"

30

One is reminded of the words of Maj. Gen. Joshua L. Chamberlain: "They will come together again under a higher bidding, and will know their place and name. This army will live, and live on, so long as soul shall answer soul...."

In the fall of 1999 I was invited to autograph my books at a local Visitor's Welcome Center. I met a young woman who was a student at a local college. She came specifically to ask about some experiences she and some friends had on the Gettysburg Battlefield. I asked her to write them down, which she did: four full single-spaced, typed pages of them! Her experiences have occurred at different sites, so you will hear from her again.

Her first paranormal experience was in June 1995. A group of students had gone on a "ghost hunt" to Devil's Den and the Triangular Field one night. They were extremely disappointed that the Triangular Field did not yield up its spirits to them, and so they began to walk back to their cars parked on the other side of Devil's Den. Partway back, a group of them stopped and turned around to notice a small, stocky individual carrying a knapsack and smoking. He was near Smith's Battery, and so the woman just assumed that he was a Union soldier, perhaps a reenactor...except for the fact that, as they watched, he began to slowly become translucent, then "just faded away."

There were other people standing over in Devil's Den. One of the students called to them and asked if one of their friends had wandered over to where they stood. "No," was the reply. It then struck the group just what had happened. It was the first time the young lady had ever experienced a paranormal event. But it would not be the last.

Almost exactly a year later, in June 1996, she and a friend returned to the Triangular Field. It was late afternoon and they were walking up through Devil's Den when suddenly they were startled by a sharp explosion just in front of them. Topping the hill at Smith's Battery, they realized the source—an old "clunker" of a car, backfiring—and laughed it off.

Continuing toward the Triangular Field, they heard booming noises coming from the woods and just assumed it was the old car backfiring again. Then they heard another series of sharp reports, different from the backfiring, coming from deeper in the woods. Having been to reenactments, and having just heard the backfiring of a car, she realized that the sound was different, that it was the distinct booming roar of cannons firing. It lasted for nearly 30 seconds, she wrote, perhaps a phantom battery its ghostly artillerists fooled into returning the fire of a much more modern invention.

They walked to the woods on the other side of the three-sided field to discover the source of the noise, and found none. But as they stood there, peering across the wall at the woods that witnessed the several charges of the Texans and Georgians, they heard the unmistakable sound of human footsteps walking toward them. She looked for squirrels—usually the obvious source of noise in the woods—but, as she wrote, "the sound was distinguishably two-footed and not four-footed. The footsteps came closer and closer and finally we both screamed and ran down the hill to where the car was parked."

By the end of her first year at college, she had a reputation for her Gettysburg paranormal experiences, even though many of her sojourns to Gettysburg produced nothing extraordinary. But she did have enough strange experiences that she frankly admitted to becoming accustomed to paranormal events that would drive her friends screaming in panic to their cars. Her most recent experience at the Triangular Field, however, sent chills down even her spine.

It occurred on the evening that I met her and her friend. Afterward, they decided they were going to visit Gettysburg. In fact, they invited me to accompany them, but I was tired after a long day and declined. Perhaps I should have accepted their invitation.

Arriving in Gettysburg, they drove immediately to the Triangular Field. Like the other times she had been there in winter and fall, the battlefield was deserted. It was about 8:00 p.m., very dark and cold. They were about to get out of the car when she decided not to, because she suddenly had a premonition, a very bad feeling about leaving the vehicle. Her girlfriend wanted to get out, but as she was about to open the door, there came through the night a reminder of the horrid, hellish reality the Triangular Field was once witness to: piercing through the dark and into their car came a scream, emanating from a human throat, tortured by unbearable pain.

Realizing what they had just heard, she drove away rapidly. Along the twisted, darkened road they went until her friend asked her if she had heard it, too. Of course, was the reply, but her friend insisted—did it sound like this?— and mimicked the dreadful cry so perfectly that it made the writer of the letter scream herself.

They decided to drive to Cemetery Ridge. As they drove, her friend asked if she could imagine what kind of pain a person must have been in to make that kind of sound. They parked the car in front of the High Water Mark monument, the huge bronze open book upon which the names of the units that participated in the repulse of Pickett's Charge are inscribed. But her friend was extremely uncomfortable; she kept saying that it felt as if she was being watched and kept turning in her seat to look over her shoulder.

Her hand, on which she had surgery earlier that year, began to itch and burn. As they were returning to college on Route 30, she began to complain more and more about her hand. Looking at it, she realized that her hand was inexplicably beginning to swell.

Halfway home, the hand had swollen so much that the young woman had to remove her rings and watch. Knowing her friend was Catholic, she pulled into the lot of a Catholic Church. They entered the house of God, found the Holy Water font, and sprinkled some on the hand at the spot where the pain was most intense. Immediately, the pain subsided and the swelling began to go down.

Was this young woman of the current century suffering a "sympathy" wound for a soldier from the last century? They say it happens to those who have particularly intense, emotional, religious experiences. Those wounds are called stigmata, and emulate the wounds of One who also sacrificed Himself for us to prove that Death itself can be conquered. You hear it in the words of the Civil War soldiers' favorite song: "As He died to make men holy, let us die to make men free...."

An attorney wrote me a letter about an unexplainable experience he had in July 1999. He admitted that he had previous encounters with ghosts in Bucks County, Pennsylvania, but also pointed out that, as is natural for one in his profession, he keeps a skeptical eye on everything he encounters. In spite of his skepticism, his experience at Gettysburg confounded him.

He also reenacts Civil War battles as a hobby, which is why he was here in July 1999. He explained that they were told to "stand down" for the afternoon, which gave them the opportunity to visit the battlefield. Three men of their unit spent about four hours visiting sites on the field, and they finally ended up at the monument to the 145th Pennsylvania. He has been drawn to it ever since two friends of his felt "presences" there, and one caught a glimpse of a phantom Union soldier in the woods watching them.

The 145th Pennsylvania monument is in one of the most secluded areas of the battlefield. Just past the Triangular Field is a crossroads where you can only turn left. That takes you through the area where attacks that were part of the Confederate assaults through the Triangular Field passed. The road goes down into the valley of Plum Run, across the old trolley track bed, and upwards, curving to the right. At the top of the hill you can overlook the Rose Farm house. Some maps show hundreds of dead Confederates buried between that hilltop and the Rose Farm. Despite this, no one has done much paranormal research at the Rose Farm. An after-dark visit to the farm is likely to produce the famous "orb" photos, or a superabundance of electronic voice phenomena—voices recorded on tape some say, of the dead. It is very still out there, very dark and quiet....

The very first ghost story about the Battle of Gettysburg comes from the Union troops themselves. Marching toward Gettysburg through the long, dark night of July 1-2, the leading elements of the Army of the Potomac's Fifth Corps see something in the distance ahead. It must be more of that weird mist they keep seeing on their night marches. No. It is moving! It is a rider...on a huge white horse. He lets them get close, then moves swiftly, but somehow without his horse galloping, farther ahead of the column, seemingly almost protective of the soldiers behind him. Once, some of them think they get a closer look and are a little befuddled. He is dressed in a military uniform all right, but it is a uniform out of the last century. They make out a flowing cape and a tricorn hat, and... "By God," says one. He looks hard into the darkness ahead. He, and now several others are sure of what they see. It is General George Washington, leading them into Pennsylvania in pursuit of the Rebels who wish to tear his country asunder. The word goes back down through the lines, and men strain to see at the head of the column, the emissary from the spirit-world here to help them. By the next day, their omen has passed through the army and it is taken as a sign of victory to come....

As they stood in their reenactor uniforms at the monument, the attorney began to tell the youngest member of the group a little about what happened to the unit on July 2, 1863. The conversation turned to Robert E. Lee, and then to Lee's hero and relative by marriage, George Washington. His comments, true to his lawyer's profession, were frank: that Washington actually was not such a good combat general since he lost most of his battles and found himself in trouble quite a bit on the battlefield. He was, however, an excellent administrator and personally courageous almost beyond belief. The conversation concluded with a discussion of Lee.

They returned to their car to continue their tour, but after turning the key several times, the car would not start. They checked the battery, starter, and other parts, which all seemed fine. Still, the car refused to start. About an hour later a woman and her husband stopped to lend assistance. While the husband fiddled under the hood, she walked over to the monument to the 145th Pennsylvania and, as he put it, "grabbed on to it."

In a few minutes she returned.

"What did you say about Washington?" she asked.

The men looked back and forth at each other in amused disbelief. She pointed directly at the attorney and asked, "What did *you* say about Washington?"

Shocked, he told her what he had said about his generalship. Then she told them that the ghosts of the 145th were mad that he had said that, and that one in particular refused to "release" the car until he apologized.

Desiring to get back into town before dark, he readily apologized. The woman paused for a minute and said that they still would not release the car.

Still the skeptic, he tried to rationalize the breakdown. It was an older car with high mileage. They waited and waited for a park ranger to come along, but none did, so the couple offered to drive the younger man into town to retrieve his car. After dropping the young man off, the couple returned— they said, "to protect" those left on this remote section of the battlefield— but the young man got lost in returning to the secluded site, and so they spent several more hours waiting. The woman kept telling them that she was seeing soldiers in the woods, including the one who would not "release" the car. The lawyer wrote that he had seen nothing the whole time, but there were some strange smells wafting by, virtually in the middle of nowhere on the battlefield.

Cooking beef they smelled while waiting; and perfume; and, perhaps not so surprisingly, rotten meat—like bad bologna, he wrote—an odor he likened to one he had smelled before, in the Philadelphia morgue locker. The woman said "they" still would not release their car. His one friend, in a conciliatory gesture to the spirit, tried to surrender himself to the apparitions in the area. Suddenly, branches rained down from the trees and nearly brained him.

The young man finally showed up, and they went into town to get help. They had no luck finding any police but stopped at the Borough office building and happened to run into Mayor William Troxell who was just leaving a meeting.

Typical of our mayor, he asked the men what was wrong, and if h
A few calls by the mayor himself, and a tow truck appeared. (Try d
big city!)

Returning to the vehicle, it still would not start, and so they t
Gettysburg. On the ride in, the attorney said to his friend several times that, once they get off the battlefield, watch the car start.

Mackley's Exxon is one of the longest established service stations in the area, and the first one on the way into town from the battlefield on business Route 15. The tow truck dropped off the car for service, and the owner, Ray Mackley, came out to look at the vehicle. He opened the hood and told the attorney to turn the key. Without Ray touching a thing, the car started. They drove back to the campsite, got their equipment, and left Gettysburg. According to his letter, the car has started fine ever since.

His fellow reenactors swear that he stirred up the spirits. Several other friends who have had paranormal experiences agree. He has questioned mechanics and they have given all the possible mechanical reasons why the car would not have started, but, they add, even after he managed to get the car going, it should have had problems again afterward.

The last few lines of the letter ask my opinion on the matter. Like the good lawyer he apparently is, he tries to persuade the juror: "I would hope your opinion is mechanical, and not spiritual, to what occurred."

Sorry.

The battlefield is supposed to be haunted. Houses are haunted; fields and graveyards are haunted; sometimes whole areas have the haunted stigma about them: a certain hollow, or landmark. Ghosts cross international boundaries. The Plain of Jars in Vietnam was haunted—neither side would fight there. Vehicles are sometimes haunted. People, sometimes, are haunted.

And there is at least one monument on the Gettysburg Battlefield that is said to be haunted. The monument to the 2nd Company, Andrews Sharpshooters, Massachusetts Volunteers, located at the big curve in the Loop has, for years, had the reputation of being...how shall I put it?...animated.

Coming around the curve at night, headlights hit the back of the statue, which is startling enough, to see the glowing white back of what is obviously a soldier, crouched in a firing position. What is bizarre is that some people swear that he turns around to face you.

Of course that cannot be true. The monument is stone and stone is as solid and unmoving a substance as the earth can produce. There have to be very special conditions in order for the molecules in solid stone to release their bonding upon one another. We know some of the conditions—like extreme heat below the surface of the earth—but do we know all the conditions that could turn solid stone into a malleable puppet as a plaything for the dead?

...eceived a letter in 1997 from a woman who, with two friends, had come to ...ttysburg in October to partake of some of the fall festivities abundant in the area. They went out to Devil's Den and began exploring. Her friend was taking pictures and suddenly mentioned that her camera was acting funny. The man that was with them began telling the stories of camera failures at the site. Our letter-writer got a little upset and thought that he was making some of it up and trying his best to scare her. As it turned out, she would not need him to frighten her.

Later that night, they took a ghost tour, and she heard from the guide stories of cameras failing at Devil's Den.

Over dinner, they decided to return to Devil's Den that same night. They bought a new roll of film and new batteries. About 9:00 p.m. they arrived at Crawford Avenue, which runs directly into the Den. She stopped and took a picture. No problem. They drove to the parking area and tried another shot. Everything seemed fine.

They drove deeper into the Den. She decided to try another shot. The flash failed. She tried another. The shutter release button stuck hard and would not let her take another picture. Frustrated, she set the camera down. It began to rewind itself.

They continued their drive up the hill through the Den, past the Triangular Field, and through the once deadly Wheatfield, relaxing, beginning to chuckle now about the unexplainable effects wreaked upon the camera. As they passed the once reddened field of wheat which changed hands so many times on the afternoon of July 2, her male friend began to say out loud, "I am not here to cause you boys any trouble. After all, my family is from the South. There is Southern blood from Tennessee in my veins."

The car began its turn to the left to enter "The Loop." Out of the corners of their eyes they all caught something. The headlights had not hit it yet, but the statue—the one of the soldier from Massachusetts with its back to you—was lit with an unearthly, bluish-green glow from top to bottom. As their headlights hit it, they swear, "It turned at the shoulder and looked at us!" Needless to say, the gas pedal was used liberally on the way back into town.

And finally, at the door of the *Ghosts of Gettysburg Candlelight Walking Tours®* office, someone left the following note:

To Whom it may concern,

We came to Gettysburg in July 1998 for the first time. We loved it!

This little chip of rock, I took from the triangle close to devil's den. Since we've taken the rock, bad stuff has been happening to us. The last straw for us was last night. Someone hit our 1995 Taurus and it demolished the back door. I ask that whomever gets this letter, please [underlined 3 times] take this back to the triangle. It will be bad luck, forever cursed!

Thanks, Anonymous

The rock was missing!

EDEN AFIRE

The sleeping and the dead
Are but as pictures.
 —Macbeth, Act II, Sc. i.

Anyone visiting the National Cemetery at Gettysburg must remember that almost every soldier, North or South, killed in the Battle of Gettysburg was buried twice. The first entombment was where he fell, on a Gettysburg farmer's land, or some Gettysburg woman's doorstep. They were buried by their comrades in arms, if they fell near where their own lines were located, or by the farmers or the women themselves with feeble tools in backyard gardens in town because the soil was loose, hideous plantings destined, eventually, to bloom with an even more hideous crop. Since the Union Army remained in possession of the field after the battle, Federal soldiers sometimes helped to bury and identify their comrades. Dead Federals, buried by their friends, were often more readily identified when it came time for reburial in the National Cemetery. Confederates buried by Union soldiers sometimes could not be identified.

Markers often were temporary wooden headboards with identities (if they could be discerned) scratched on them in pencil or charcoal. Some just said things like, "38 Tigers ANV" meaning that 38 beloved sons and fathers and husbands and brothers from Louisiana who fought with the Army of Northern Virginia, now mangled to death by war's grisly hand, were all buried in this one spot.

The armies marched away. Rains came and went. Grave markers were knocked down by cattle grazing. It was not unusual for a Gettysburg child to walk out into their garden or farm field after a particularly heavy rain, and be confronted with the grim, sloughing visage of a formerly patriotic warrior, or a skeletal hand and arm poking its eerie way through the thin topsoil as if homesick for the light of day. From that day on, visions of what eventually awaits us all, roamed at will like grim stalkers through the days and nights of those particular children of Gettysburg.

Irate citizens wrote letters to their legislators in the hot months after the battle: bodies were rising out of their temporary graves as if it were some bizarre counterfeit of the Great Resurrection Day; the smell has descended upon Gettysburg again, indescribable; please, Governor Curtin, can you do something?

Like all good politicians, the Honorable Andrew Curtin rode down from Harrisburg to inspect the source of his constituents' complaints. He, like everyone who saw and smelled the post-battle effluvium, was appalled. He delegated one

David Wills, a Gettysburg attorney, to purchase land for the collection and proper burial of the loyal sons of the Union who perished in the great conflagration. Wills logically bought seventeen acres right next to the existent Evergreen Cemetery and reburials began on October 27, 1863. A local man, Samuel Weaver, won out against all other bidders to exhume and rebury the bodies at $1.59 apiece. Now we know exactly what a grateful government thinks its "sainted dead" are worth; consider that the next time we wish to go to war.

With a few short winter breaks while the cruel winds on the battlefield froze the ground solid, the reburials began again and were completed by March 18, 1864. The National Cemetery was dedicated, of course, by President Abraham Lincoln on November 19, 1863, before all reburials were complete. A final total of Civil War burials was once determined as 3,706, out of which 1664 are nameless, but identified as to which state they came from. Nine hundred and seventy-nine lie in their own sections under mere numbered, granite blocks, having sacrificed not only every vestige of their identity from place of birth to the very names given them by their parents, but their own personal futures and their unborn descendants' lives as well. These soldiers, "known but to God," are the true heroes of Gettysburg.[1]

Of course, in spite of what the National Park Service told people for years— that there were no more bodies left buried out in the fields—there were. The figures just did not add up. The number of known killed in the battle (or even a good estimate), minus the numbers exhumed and reburied did not balance. Estimates are anywhere from 300 to 800 soldiers unaccounted for. As well, they keep emerging, like the poor soul found a few years back at the middle Railroad Cut. He was buried in one special, reserved grave in the National Cemetery, as will be all the others found in future years.

A walk through the National Cemetery is usually a contemplative journey into one's own thoughts. If one thinks of men who had been through the horror of battle and of this as their final rest, it is a calming place.

We thought that the cavalryman who once stalked the National Cemetery had finally found his rest. But apparently, we were wrong. There seems to be another—or perhaps more than one—entity that continues to walk through the cemetery...and eternity.

A young lady wrote to me and told of a stroll she and her mother took just before they closed the National Cemetery for the evening. As they were walking, suddenly from behind them came the sound of footsteps pacing theirs. They turned to see who it was, but in the dim, dusky light they could see no one, although the footfalls seemed very close.

As they continued their walk, a park ranger vehicle entered the cemetery, making one final swing around the road to make sure everyone was out before the gates were closed at dusk. The young lady and her mother decided to turn back since it was a long way around the cemetery and they probably would be turned back by the ranger anyway. Surprisingly (or, since it was Gettysburg, not so surprisingly) they did not run into whoever it was that was trailing them before.

Then, while walking back, they heard them again—the soft footfalls trailing them from the area they had just left. Finally they reached the gate. They turned to see the ranger vehicle lights illuminate the area where they had heard the steps. Nothing.

I get hundreds of letters and phone calls from people who believe they have had a paranormal experience on this great plain of death we call Gettysburg. Usually I store them away for future reference, or for some archive of paranormal events, should anyone like to look at them in the years after I am gone. Sometimes, however, I find just fragments of notes of phone conversations or a page of a three-page letter, the rest of it misfiled.

Typed notes found in my East Cemetery Hill file state, "Also heard footsteps following them at dusk from E. Cemetery Hill to Stevens Knoll; also artillery or wagon wheels to the east as they returned and the banging of drums. Could see, however, a campfire in the field and what appeared to be a lantern swinging back and forth. Looking behind them they saw a candle light, & so they ran to the top of Cem. Hill & Baltimore St."

On the weekend of the anniversary of the battle, and coincidentally, the Fourth of July, 2000, a reenactor and a couple of his friends came into the *Ghosts of Gettysburg Candlelight Walking Tours®* headquarters. I was standing next to the ticket desk and he approached. On his face he wore a strange half-smile. We introduced ourselves and he began his story with, "I'm a person who doesn't believe anything I can't see or touch."

At first, I thought that he was going to tell me that he did not believe any of the stories in my books, or that I was making them all up, or that the people I have interviewed or who have written me letters were all crazy. And that may have been exactly what he would have told me...if he had run into me just an hour or so before he had his own experience.

He said he and his young friend had been walking in the National Cemetery. It was late dusk and they were on their way out, when something told him to turn around. Behind him stood a Confederate, nearer the gravestones than to him. He described the man in excruciating detail for several minutes, right down to the filth covering him. I fully expected him to tell me how, after "playing" a ghost and trying to scare the Union reenactor telling the story, the Confederate reenactor joined the rest for a good laugh and left the Cemetery with them.

But the Confederate never left.

The man who stood before me told of how they had stopped, taken a step or two toward the Rebel to get a better look at him, and watched him dematerialize right before their eyes.

"You can ask him," he said, pointing to the young man, nodding his head from a few feet away. "He was as real as you are standing here in front of me...and he just disappeared." The smile he wore I now recognized as belonging to one who had just had an epiphany. He had been as good a skeptic as anyone, until an hour ago. Now what?

CLIMBING TO GOLGOTHA

He that dies pays all debts.
—William Shakespeare, *The Tempest*

By early morning of July 2, 1863, the digging and chopping and hacking was almost unbearable. The men of Johnson's Division, Ewell's Corps, had been listening to it since dark of the night before. After driving the Yankees like cattle through the town the previous afternoon, they had wanted to continue their assault up the hill ahead before the Federals got it. But for some reason, unexplained to them, they were halted.

General Robert E. Lee had directed Lt. Gen. Richard Ewell to advance and take the heights "if practicable." Ewell, left to his own discretion, felt like playing it safe.

The men of Steuart's Brigade were especially anxious. Excavating was going on just about a mile from them as they stood in line on the rolling farmlands behind the stone house of Daniel Lady, and they knew what that meant. The hated Yankees, thousands of their enemy, were clearing fields of fire, building breastworks with the fallen logs, and carving lunettes out of raw earth in front of their artillery pieces. The veteran Rebel infantrymen had seen, firsthand, infantry assaults up a hill against entrenched positions chewed to pieces. Cleared fields before breast-high earth and log works became a meat grinder, and when the defenders' artillery spewed canister— the thumb-sized lead and iron balls blasting out of the cannon's mouths— they could expect to see men liquefied before their very eyes, literally torn to bits, arms from torsos, entrails scooped and flung from bodies, heads carved in half, by the indifferent clots of metal. The simplest private in Johnson's Division knew that they were going to have to assault that hill eventually and each minute given to the Federals to entrench would sacrifice more Southern lives.

By 4:00 p.m. on July 2, Robert E. Lee's battle plan was beginning to unfold.

He saw that the Union line was, in military parlance, an "interior" line. Shaped like a giant fish hook, communications and reinforcements could be moved rapidly from one end of the line, across the inside of the curve, to the other end, if either became threatened. Lee's plan then was to neutralize that advantage with a simple tactic: attack both ends of the Union line simultaneously. It made sense: a successful attack upon Culp's Hill would cut the Baltimore Pike—a major retreat route for the Federal Army back to Washington; success against the Round Top flank would cut the Taneytown road, a second retreat route. The Confederates already had possession of the Emmitsburg Road. Lee's battle plan was brilliant in its simplicity.

So it would seem that its execution would be easy as well. Ewell was to launch his attack at the sound of the guns on the other end of the field. Though others in Johnson's Division heard the guns clearly enough to count the discharges, Ewell did not order his men to move until nearly 6:00 p.m.; they didn't reach the base of Culp's Hill for another hour and forty-five minutes.[1]

Through no intentional plan on the part of Ewell, the delay was actually fortunate.

As the fighting raged on the other side of the field—at Little Round Top— Union soldiers were pulled from their well prepared trenches on Culp's Hill at about 6:30 p.m. to aid in the fighting to the south. Only one Union brigade of about 1,400 men and officers was left on Culp's Hill. But they were under the command of a particularly experienced officer.

Brigadier General George S. Greene, at 63 years of age, no doubt looked to the young men of his brigade like Methuselah. He bent back his line—"refused" it, according to the tactical term—and had the youngsters from New York dig another trench perpendicular to the ones they held.

When the fighting began it was nearly dark.

Confederates waded Rock Creek holding muskets and cartridge boxes above the waist-deep water, but that was just the beginning of their problems. That side of Culp's Hill was rock-strewn, with cuts and boulders and a couple of cliff-like escarpments. One of the units coming into battle knew where they were going only by following musket flashes. It must have been horrifying: fighting first through brambles and over fallen logs, tripping, stumbling, not knowing where to go until the night lights up with pinprick musket-flashes, suddenly beautiful, but just as suddenly deadly. One man fires in the darkness ahead of you, then you fire, then three men fire at your muzzle flash and you hear the bullets zip by, then ten fire at their muzzle flashes, and so on in the deadly sport. One unit tragically fired into their own comrades after seeing their muskets' flash. Widows and orphans were being created because Ewell's attack got underway too late.

The "Old Man," Greene, seemed to be everywhere at once. He kept to his mount and rode the fiery lines in the dark. The commander of reinforcements, for which he had called, arrived apparently when the firing was loudest—Greene had to write his own name on paper and hand it to the officer to identify himself. But while the old man and his young charges held tenaciously to the breastworks for two hours, Confederates found their way into the other trenches abandoned by Federal troops sent to Little Round Top.[2]

Years later, aging Southern veterans of the fighting would reminisce about how close they had come to turning the world upside down, here on this very spot. They were a carbine's shot from the Baltimore Pike and the rear of the Union Army, from attacking all the noncombatants behind the lines and throwing them back into the rear of the combat troops, causing the utmost in confusion and panic. In the dark, who knows what they could have done.

But the onyx of that July night made ghosts out of the eerie moving shadows among the trees on Culp's Hill, and they were suspicious. No one just walks into the enemy's trenches in a combat zone—into their smoldering campfires with coffee half-cooked and playing cards in mid-deal—without a fight. The Confederates halted and sent out scouts to find the treacherous Yankees. They needed a better look before they would feel comfortable enough—if you ever feel comfortable in battle—to advance. No doubt more than one thought about the advantage some higher ground with a view would give them, or how one of those crazy balloons they had seen operating on the Peninsula the year before would allow them to see over the trees and this hill before them....

So, the very delay that helped the Confederates gain access to the Union trenches also brought on the darkness and confusion that stopped them.

Overnight the Federal troops returned, and the fight began anew with the dawn. Any advantage the Confederates might have had in the dark the night before was lost, evaporating like the hazy night mist that embraces the wooded sides of Culp's Hill to this very day.

But people still came to the hill, years after the battle and the war, to see where immortal deeds were done by mortal men. In 1864 an organization was formed and incorporated as the Gettysburg Battlefield Memorial Association. They began to purchase battleground to save for posterity; the first purchases were Culp's Hill, East Cemetery Hill, and part of the summit of Little Round Top. Beginning in 1878, monuments and markers began to be placed upon the field.

In 1895 the War Department of the United States assumed jurisdiction of land purchased by the Gettysburg Battlefield Memorial Association. Soldiers who came after the soldiers who fought there realized that, in order to see the importance of Culp's Hill without denuding it of historically correct trees, they had to build a tower. Made out of steel, it stands today, just topping the trees, and gives a shocking view of how close the Confederates came to the Baltimore Pike. If the Confederates had only had the view of the Yankee lines from that tower at the battle....

In June 1994, I received a letter from a woman whose family had visited the battlefield in April. They toured the fields of carnage during the day, but she felt drawn to visit them again at dusk. They sat and watched the spectacular sunset afforded by the view from Little Round Top, then continued around the battlefield to Culp's Hill. Once they entered the dark enchantment of the fought-over woods, the woman began to get the sensation of movement through the shadowy trees out of her peripheral vision. It must have looked very much to her like what the Confederates saw and feared: a dangerous enemy moving with stealth through the trees just yards away. But like the vision the Confederates had thirteen decades past, the movement she saw was not real either, but merely walking shadows. By the time they reached Spangler's Spring, it was completely dark.

They drove their vehicle to the right at Spangler's Spring and began to climb the winding road up Culp's Hill. Just to the right were remnants of some of the breastworks dug 131 years before by the desperate Union soldiers, abandoned, taken over by the Rebels, and retaken in the dark by the Federals pouring in from the modern visitor's left.

Suddenly, from the woods to the left, the entire family saw a bright, white flash of light. Startled, the woman said, "what was that?" Her husband had seen it, as did the children. Their first thought was a headlight, but it was right near them in the trees and seemed to be moving, as if, she explained, someone had thrown fireworks. No one could explain it. It defies description today. The nearest road to where they were was on the other side of the hill, out of sight of their position. They were completely perplexed.

In 1996 a family sent me a photograph of their two children at Spangler's Spring that may help to explain what the people saw.

They had brought their children to Gettysburg on the anniversary of the battle for three years running. The father, in his letter, explained that he was an amateur historian with a science background. Late in the evening on July 2, the anniversary of the fighting there, the family was exploring the Spangler's Meadow and Spring area. There had been a heavy downpour of rain before they reached their destination. The father took several photos with his new, fully automatic 35 mm camera. He was about halfway through the roll when he took a picture of his children, holding umbrellas since it had been raining, one on each side of the domed structure that houses the drinking fountain at Spangler's Spring. Then he took several other photos and finished the roll.

Some paranormalists feel that weather conditions have much to do with supernatural activity. Many believe that just before and after thunderstorms are good times to try and photograph entities or collect electronic voice phenomena, otherwise known as EVP. We know from experimentation that the "orbs" people photograph, as well as "ectoplasm" are electrically charged. Gauss meters spike when passing through areas of energy concentration, and when photos are taken, more often than not, there are the unexplainable orbs floating mysteriously in the photo.

They had purchased *Ghosts of Gettysburg* while here. When they returned home and were looking at the developed pictures, the daughter gasped at the one taken at Spangler's Spring. There, coming from the left hand edge of the photo and extending to the rail of the Spangler's Spring dome, cutting the young man's image in half, is a bright white streak, about 1/8 inch wide, and ending in a semicircle. His sister had read the stories in my book about the "Woman in White" who is seen so frequently in the fields and woods surrounding Spangler's Spring. She thought this might be her.

The father, however, was skeptical, so he took the photo and the negative to the local camera shop and photo studio. The technicians studied both. They had no explanation. Examination under magnification shows two circular areas in the streak, one with a distinct pink aura emanating from it. Since the photo was in the middle of the roll and the photos captured right before and right after have no overexposed areas, the possibility of the photographer accidentally opening the back of the camera and exposing a streak—if that can even be done without exposing the rest of the negative—is eliminated. Whatever it is, it is bright, circular, and in rapid motion, and looks like what the other family may have seen on the side of the hill that was once a wooded hell.

I had spoken with, then later received a letter from, a man who, on a business trip from Harrisburg to Pittsburgh decided to take a couple of days and visit Gettysburg. It was the beginning of May 1998, and about 8:00 p.m. when he arrived at the Culp's Hill tower. A lightning storm had just passed and subsided, so he felt safe in ascending the steel tower to view the battlefield. He spent about five minutes videotaping, then several more minutes in the contemplative quiet. He was just about to start down the stairs to his van on the ground when he heard someone start up the stairs.

He had not heard anyone drive up, but thought nothing of that; perhaps it was a walker taking the tower for a little more exercise. In fact, as he timed the pace of the individual, he realized that they were taking the steps at a good clip, not running or jogging them, but faster than normal. He also noticed that the sound of the footsteps was distinctively leather-soled shoes: not lugged hiking boots and not neoprene running shoes.

He was leaning against the steel railing on the northeast corner of the tower and so could not only hear the footfalls, but feel them vibrating through the tower's structure as well. The steps were relatively light; he estimated they belonged to a teenaged boy or remotely a woman. Being a very security-minded individual, both by natural inclination and by profession, the thought crossed his mind that there was the remote possibility that this person was ascending the tower with malevolence against a lone tourist in mind. Using his training, he assumed a good defensive position, just in case.

The footsteps stopped on the landing just below the top platform of the tower. The man waited a minute for them to continue the rest of the way, but they did not. Again, because of the lightness of step, and the hesitation of the individual to confront someone already on the tower in such a secluded place, he thought the climber might be a youthful man.

At this moment he crossed the tower platform, stopping just short of the stairs, once again leaning upon his professional defensive training. He waited, still hearing nothing from below. He finally stepped over to the entrance to the stairs, prepared to congratulate the individual upon his physical conditioning for taking the stairs at that rate. His words went unspoken: he was looking at an empty landing and beyond it, down an empty staircase.

He had absolutely no doubt of what he had heard. He hurried down the staircase to confirm that there was no one else in the vicinity. He stood at the tower's base for a few minutes. Then, a smile began to spread across his face as he finally began to realize what had just happened. Out loud, to no one except

The observation tower on Culp's Hill.

himself and whatever invisible entity had just entered this world and left it noiselessly, he said, *"That* was good, *really* good...."

He got in his vehicle and headed out the Baltimore Pike, but he could not help himself. He turned in on the road that circles Culp's Hill and drove the route again to see if he could spot anyone walking away from that tower. The roads, at 8:30 p.m. were deserted.

He revisited the tower the next morning before he left Gettysburg. Witnessing a young couple ascend and then descend the same tower, he realized that one makes considerably more noise coming down the steel steps than going up. He knew then that, if whatever it was that had visited him on the tower the day before had descended by conventional means, he certainly would have heard it.

Analyzing his experience, he discounted the power of suggestion as the cause. Anything paranormal, he would have expected to see, but "the idea that I might *hear* footsteps where there apparently were none *had simply never occurred to me!"* Informing him that a Civil War soldier's "Brogan" footwear had leather soles would not have helped explain his experience.

His confusion concerning the event may have been assuaged, however, if he had seen a letter I have in my files.

A man who is an engineer and his brother-in-law were visiting Gettysburg at the beginning of October 1997. It was a wonderfully warm day, which is usually a surprise to many people who do not realize how warm it stays in Gettysburg, often all the way into November.

They parked their car in the lot at the base of the Culp's Hill tower and climbed the stairs to the top platform. Theirs was the only car in the lot and he was a little surprised that they were the only ones there.

His brother-in-law had moved to the southeast corner of the square observation platform and the writer of the letter had moved to the northwest corner and was standing a little to the right of it at the safety wall. All of a sudden a wraith-like figure swept past him to his left. He turned to see an attractive young woman standing at the west rail. His first reaction was to wonder where she came from, since he had heard no car door close from below and had heard no footsteps on the stairs.

The man admits that, because of his natural dislike of crowds, he is usually keenly aware of the approach of others, especially in any confined space, like the platform of the tower. As well, at that moment he had a sense of "something distinctly out of the ordinary." The thought flashed through his mind: was this some kind of paranormal experience?

They did not make eye contact. He could not see her from the front, since she was staring out to the west. He remembered being surprised that she did not appear winded from the climb. He expected any minute for her boyfriend to appear. No one did.

Since he was behind her he got a chance to make some mental notes: she was Caucasian, medium height, about 5'6" he guessed, around 30 years old with shoulder-length blonde hair done in tight curls. She wore a red sweater and blue jeans. He thought she may have worn a scarf tied around her neck as well. ɪ remembered thinking, how appropriate for Gettysburg: she is wearing red, white (her blonde hair) and blue. From his description, she seemed to have the look of someone perhaps a generation earlier, possibly from the '50s. Even though she dressed casually, he remembered that she looked very "elegant and had a kind of quiet serenity." She stayed only a short time, turned to her left and walked halfway around the deck, passing behind his brother-in-law who continued peering off to the south.

Though politeness dictated to him that he should greet her since they were all sharing the same small platform eighty feet in the air, she started back down the stairs without so much as a glance at the other human beings with her. Thinking this a little too nonchalant, he moved to position himself where he could see her descending.

But he never saw her again. She did not descend the stairs. She did not leave the base of the tower. She did not enter a car. He did not hear a car door open or slam, or a car depart. He did not see, from the panoramic view the tower provides, the lovely young woman walking out of the area. She had disappeared as mysteriously as she had appeared.

The whole time the two men spent at the tower, no one else arrived in the vicinity.

The writer of the letter said nothing to his in-law until a few hours later. Finally he asked him if he had seen the lovely lady at the tower, the only other person who had visited the tower while they were there, and certainly the most striking woman they had seen all day. His in-law replied no, he had not seen anyone on the tower.

He could not believe it. He described her in great detail, her attire, her hair color, her height and age. In return, he only received an odd look from his in-law, and a reaffirmation that he was the only one on that tower to have seen the young lady, who neither announced her presence nor signaled her departure, from one world to the next.

THOSE WHO CAST NO SHADOWS

What are these,
So withered, and so wild in their attire,
That look not like th' inhabitants o' th' earth,
And yet are on 't.
—Macbeth I, iii

Some believe that Death is not just the veil drawn between this life and the next. They believe it is an impassible wall through which neither light nor sound pass. It represents extinction of the individual self; indescribable nothingness—not blackness, not blankness, not coldness nor heat nor temperateness, but no feeling of any kind. After it there are no fears, no anticipation, no joy, no hope, no time, no judgement, perhaps even no God, some believe. It is the beginning of absolute nothingness. Surely the imagination allows it, but does science? Abject nothingness—a vacuum that does not even allow for a vacuum— seems a contradiction. Beyond that concept, it is a truly dismal thought: that there is nothing beyond, and that life is spent—our toils and troubles—for absolutely nothing.

To many, "ghosts" are a manifestation of beings from beyond the end of life, which would seem a great comfort rather than a reason for fear. Unfortunately, the term "ghost" has certain baggage that comes with it—invented mostly by Hollywood—and if we would give another name to the supernatural events some have experienced, like "residual being energy," or "cross-dimensional contacts," perhaps people would be more accepting of the concept that those who have gone before us, also return.

Because, if you do not believe in ghosts, this is what you must believe: That there is an absolute vacuum, a total void that exists in some dimension, somewhere, and that death is the final closing door on everything.

There are some who deny the existence of ghosts because they refuse to believe in something they cannot see or hear or smell. What then of love and joy and honor and hope and grief and the pleasure of sacrifice for good? All are unseen and have no qualities that can be put on a scale or placed before a ruler and measured. Do they exist? Of course they do.

There are others who just do not "believe" in ghosts. Which is fine. But not "believing" in something does not make it disappear. One person's belief has nothing to do with another's reality. The paranormal experiences chronicled in my books have nothing to do with whether you believe in ghosts or not. They have to do with whether you believe in the human senses—do you believe in what you see or hear or smell or the coldness that you feel? Do you believe that others' senses operate in the same manner as yours? Of course, you do not have to "believe" in apples for them to exist. They just do.

I have also heard people—especially long term residents of Gettysburg—say, "I've lived here for forty years and I've never seen anything."

There are three misconceptions underlying that statement. First, I was never in Vietnam or the American Civil War. Am I supposed to conclude that there was never any combat action there? Just because "I" did not experience something, does not mean it did not happen. Second, "seeing" a ghost is, by far, the least common way of experiencing the paranormal, a statement backed up by several independent sociological studies. So if someone asks if you have ever "seen" a ghost, although you have had numerous paranormal experiences, to answer truthfully, you must say no. Finally, we are all sensitive to the paranormal in different degrees. You may live in a "haunted" house for thirty years and never experience anything out of the ordinary. Your niece from out of town may stay overnight and ask who was the woman in the old fashioned dress whom she saw in the hall the night before.

But Gettysburg—and other places of human destruction on a massive scale—where the souls of young men and boys were ripped from their mortal temples and those bodily temples torn apart and scattered by the hot clods of iron passing through them, retains some of the essences of those men. Many who died here were extinguished immediately, before their consciousness even knew it; many more had a few seconds to wonder where they were going to end up; some thought they were about to get better, then two weeks later succumbed disbelieving, within a half day, of infection. None was ready. Some did not even know they were dead. Some still do not....

Visitors to Gettysburg are driven over "The Railroad Cut" and told of the savage fighting there on the morning of July 1, 1863. What they may not notice, with all the National Park Service signage and the fact that the battlefield tour road runs right over one of them, is that there are actually three railroad cuts at Gettysburg. Along the railroad tracks a few hundred yards to the east of the cut that is crossed by the battlefield road is another cut, which David G. Martin in his extensive work of the first day at Gettysburg calls the eastern railroad cut. A couple hundred yards west of the "famous" cut is yet another cut, logically named by Martin the western cut. The interesting thing about them is that—like in the Sunken Road at Antietam, or behind the stone wall at Fredericksburg—modern visitors can stand in the same spot where the soldiers stood and fought, bled and died.

They also represent an excellent reference point from which one can imagine the rest of the fighting that took place there from the accounts of the participants. And fairly savage and heavy fighting it was.

The battle around the easternmost cut (remember, in 1863 there were no ties or tracks in the cuts yet since the railroad stopped at the Western Maryland Railroad Station on Carlisle Street) climaxed around 3:30 p.m., and involved some vicious fighting between Confederate infantry and the artillery of Stewart's Battery. The battery was split across the railroad cut with three guns on the north side and three on the south. Union infantry—remnants of the 6th Wisconsin—came out from the shelter of the railroad cut to support the battery.

In the artillerist's manual of the Civil War era, there is a section that discusses serving the gun with diminished numbers. Each gun was typically served by nine men, with each man having a specific duty by the numbers: No. 1 would swab and ram; No. 2 would load the powder bag and shell; No. 3 would thumb the vent and poke a hole in the bag of powder, and so on. But virtually immediately, in a hot combat situation, the gunners would begin to take casualties, so everyone had to know everyone else's job, and ended up doing two or three before the fight was over. In a well-drilled, veteran artillery battery, they would stand to their gun with minie balls thwacking off wooden wheels and ringing off the bronze barrel, or thudding hard into the soft bellies of their comrades. So when Confederates opened with a steady fire on Stewart's battery, as one eyewitness remembered, they "killed Stewart's men and horses in great numbers, but did not seem to check his fire."

But even the artillerists had to retreat eventually, as overwhelming pressure from the Confederates mounted. The last stand on that part of the field was taken by the men of the 16th Maine, in that cut. There, they tore their flag to bits rather than have it captured by the enemy.

The 147th New York Infantry did fine work helping to defend Hall's Maine Battery of artillery. They were posted just to the north of the westernmost railroad cut, lying down, firing through the wheat in the field before them at the men of the 42nd Mississippi just a hundred yards away. A captain from the 147th later noted that if a man were wounded in that location and period of the battle, he more likely to be hit in the head and killed, since they were all lying down.

The 147th fought for another 15 minutes, holding off not only the 42nd Mississippi, but the 2nd Mississippi, now working its way around their right flank. As they traded volleys with the Mississippians, sometimes as close as 100 feet, they peered through the slowly clearing powder smoke to see that their supporting infantry on their right had been withdrawn, an order they themselves had not received. The command to retire was given to their Lt. Col. Francis Miller, but before he could pass the orders on to subordinate officers, he was wounded in the head, and his horse, wild without Miller's steady hand in battle, dashed off to the rear, carrying Miller with him. Command devolved upon Major George Harney who knew nothing of the orders to pull back.

While the 147th was occupied to its front, the 55th North Carolina had worked its way around to its right. The 147th bent its right wing back to hold off this assault. But everyone knew that it could only be temporary. Worse, Hall's Battery had been ordered to withdraw. The 147th New York was all alone.

Without orders, and braver than they ought to have been, they refused to budge an inch. Assaulted from the front and right, they still held. If not for that railroad cut to their left rear, another group of Confederates, with Hall's Battery gone, would have advanced upon that end of their line.

Finally, a galloper brings the word to retire. There was no time for formality, now. Harney called out the command, "In retreat, double quick, run." The men rose from their prone position and, having rested while the Confederates were advancing, surely outran their pursuers. Most of the men passed the railroad cuts to the north. A large number, however, used the middle cut as refuge, but found it crowded with retreating men and wounded who had crawled to it. One of the 147th who was in the cut heard the Rebel minie balls zip over the top. Finally Confederates loomed over them and captured large numbers of Federals in the cut. Soon it would be the Confederates' turn.

The 6th Wisconsin, part of the famed Iron Brigade, had taken a position parallel to and about 100 yards south of the Chambersburg Pike facing the middle railroad cut. Soon they marched across the Pike and engaged the enemy. Able to rest their muskets on a convenient fence, they stopped the advance of the Confederates into the town of Gettysburg and saved a good number of the 147th New York, retreating before them. The Rebels turned to face the fire from the 6th; some sought shelter in the middle railroad cut.

The only problem was, as any modern visitor to the cut can see, the sides are too high and steep to act as breastworks. So, a large body of infantrymen in the cut, with the exception of the ends of the line where the cut is low, are effectively out of the fight. Confederate officers, realizing this, ordered a retreat.

Rufus Dawes, commander of the 6th Wisconsin, saw what was happening and ordered his men to advance, supported on his left by other Union regiments. The advance was brutal. The 6th Wisconsin would lose a man for every step they advanced: 180 men to advance 175 paces. Once they reached the cut, the fighting was hand-to-hand, and the cry rose from the Federals for the Confederates in the cut to throw down arms and surrender. A small contingent of Federals blocked the eastern exit from the cut. The bottle was corked and the Confederates had no choice but to give up.

Some escaped, of course. One group made it through the western railroad cut. All in all, the battle around the three cuts was a wild affair with groups of men, large and small, making their way to and from the temporary shelter the cuts represented. As the years progressed after that one fabled day in July 1863, nothing like that swirling, moving combat was ever seen in those placid fields again...at least, nothing of this world.

A U.S. Navy veteran, a reenactor who portrays a Union general officer, was visiting Gettysburg for the reenactment in 1995. He and some friends had gone out to the railroad cut one night around the anniversary of the fighting there exactly one hundred and thirty-two years earlier. Their friends were frank about the fact that they were "ghost hunting," as they called it. (The term "ghost hunting" is so benign. Some believe that what they were doing is seeking out the spiritual remnants of the men killed there, like one would locate a grave and physically exhume a corpse, then pick it apart and go over it to gain certain knowledge from it. Paranormal investigators take it that seriously.)

The reenactor knew the history of the fighting in the area; that, of course, can be gleaned from many books about the topic. What he was not prepared for were the things not found in most books: illogical, impossible things that continue to occur, long after the battle has been over.

They exited their van near the statue of General Wadsworth. He began to walk out into the field near the railroad cut, and had not gone twenty feet when it felt like he had walked into a deep freeze. The hair stood on his arms. His unconscious reaction was to back off, return to the statue and sit at its base.

Taking a deep breath to compose himself, he sat for several minutes. Just as things seemed to be calming down, his attention was drawn to a strange movement in the cornfield before him. He peered into the darkness at what appeared to be a desperate group of figures running at the double quick, toward the railroad cut.

"In retreat, double quick, run!" Was the call still echoing down through time to those for whom time matters not? Were those who cast no shadows still obeying the ancient order? Are they doomed, on the anniversary of their own extinction, to hear and obey the command, over, and over, and over in the same fields, forever?

Some of the women with the group had come back to the van, visibly upset at something else they had seen and felt, out where the mists play tag like lost and lonely lovers in the sylvan fields of death. They got into the van, and left the area.

Not happy to leave well enough alone, the reenactor returned with several other people who wanted to experience what was going on at the railroad cut that dark anniversary. This time they parked about a hundred or so feet from the bridge spanning the middle cut. The man volunteered to lead the ladies to the bridge.

Fifty feet from the bridge he got the strange notion that they were being watched. Suddenly he felt it again—that damp, flesh-numbing cold, surrounding, embracing him again, like what one must feel if suddenly lowered into a grave.

He raised his hands palms forward and walked through the darkness toward the cut. Three more steps, and it was like he had hit an icy wall with his hands. The women noticed his reaction and asked if he had felt something. He nodded yes and described the feeling. They decided they had had enough and began to leave.

As they approached the van, he turned and looked back at the cut. There, at the crest of the bridge, two shadowy figures stood, watching them. They ran now, to the van. He immediately flicked the headlights on high beam. As they struck the bridge the headlights illuminated...nothing. The figures were gone, melted back into the past where they have always belonged, using Time as their camouflage.

He said he suddenly felt as if they were not welcome. They drove back to the campsite. In his letter he said that the experiences were so bizarre and vivid that, in case there was some misunderstanding on the part of those from the "other side," he refuses to wear his Civil War period uniform on the field of battle here at Gettysburg anymore.

Could it be the fact that to be in any of the "Cuts," is to be literally underground? If there are such things as psychic emanations when humans are in mortal stress, in an open field, most would dissipate into the air. In a building, when one dies, there are walls to receive whatever energy is surrendered by the human form on its quick passage into the next realm. But underground, are they captured within the earth or rock outcroppings? Could there still be minor echoes of those emotions ringing off the walls of the sliced earth at the railroad cuts?

View from within the Railroad Cut looking to the east.

In July 1999, a man and his wife visited Gettysburg for the first time. They approached the town from the north, and stopped in the parking lot of the Adams County Prison to inspect some nearby monuments. Unable to find a tourist center, they drove around rather aimlessly until they stopped at the restaurant adjacent to General Lee's Headquarters. After eating, they toured Lee's Headquarters. The man purchased a reproduction Confederate kepi, a few minie balls for souvenirs, and a copy of *Ghosts of Gettysburg*. When the clerk handed him change, he felt a chill roll up his spine and he broke out in a "cold sweat."

A diabetic, he thought that perhaps his sugar was out of balance, but testing it with a kit in the car confirmed that it was fine. It was a typically hot July day, but he could not shake the chill that hit him in General Lee's Headquarters; even his wife noticed that he had "goosebumps."

Stranger than the permeating chill that invaded his body was the fact that, even though they had never been to Gettysburg before, he suddenly knew all the turns, all the roads they drove, the regiments to whom the monuments were dedicated, even before they arrived at them. It was, he said, almost as if he had grown up around Gettysburg. A tour map they had obtained remained unopened on the seat next to him.

He assured me in his letter that he did not feel as if he were possessed, or were some soldier reincarnated. He felt that the theory of "ancestral memory"— that animals are born with certain "programs" inherited biologically, and that humans can pass intense memories of fear to their offspring—did not apply to him in this case.

The only thing that helped him understand what might have happened occurred when they arrived home. As he emptied out his pockets, with his change was an odd coin. He picked it up, and realized that when he got his change at General Lee's Headquarters, he had been given an Indian Head Penny, dated 1862, minted during the Civil War.

We call them relics. Sometimes they are the bones of a saint, or pieces of wood or nails from the True Cross. We venerate them because we feel as if we gain some sort of power or healing from them. So it seems with our own Civil War: we seek bits of uniform, or buttons or equipment; we seek the weapons they used, wondering if this musket or bayonet ever killed a man. Bullets are especially sought after since they are inexpensive and the most deadly thing for sale. Did this huge minie ball ever enter someone's body, or arm, or leg, and take their life? We are curious, fascinated that such an inanimate piece of metal—so soft it can be easily scratched with a fingernail—can extinguish that most precious, noble gift from God, a human life.

Mollie Back is one of our company's senior guides, having led hundreds of tours. With all those tours under her belt, you would think that she would be pretty jaded at the strange, unexplainable things that occur on her tours. Yet there is always the ability of the paranormal to surprise and amaze even those of us so close to it here in Gettysburg.

She had just finished a tour along Seminary Ridge and was standing in the parking lot across from General Lee's Headquarters talking to her customers before they left for their motels. It was a warm, sultry, summer night, much like the one the wounded soldiers struck down in the first day's fighting must have suffered through. Eventually, only two or three of Mollie's customers remained, and they were about to leave when suddenly their eyes were caught by something at the edge of the woods where Maj. Gen. John F. Reynolds took his last breath of sulfur-filled air.

From the woods through which the Iron Brigade advanced, then retreated, followed by surging Confederates, came a strange, flashing line of lights. The color ranged from light blue to navy blue. They began to "fire at will," as

Mollie recalled, at about two flashes per second, right down the line. She haltingly tried to explain it off as, perhaps, methane or swamp gas, but, of course, that gives off a somewhat steady glow—eerie, but not flashing "like someone had lined up thirty or so flashlights and set them off one at a time...only all blue."

Ghostly gunfire? Apparitional artillerists? "There could be a thousand explanations," Mollie said in an interview about the event. There could be.

But there could also be only one....

And finally, again from Mollie who was taking another Seminary Ridge Tour. Betty Roche, a woman on her tour, supplied Mollie with two gifts: one a relic from the battle, and another the gift of knowledge about the human mind.

Betty had experienced the paranormal before. She and her daughter took a walk after dark to the Peace Light Memorial, and were sitting on the steps of the monument enjoying the moonlit view, beyond the Mummasburg Road past the site of the Forney Farm, across the two-mile wide spot of ground where about 15,000 Federal and Confederate troops became casualties. They decided to walk around to the back of the monument, into the dark, wooded area near where the men of Iverson and Ramseur and O'Neal began their ill-fated charges upon the Union line along Oak Ridge. From the trees behind the Peace Light Memorial advanced a Confederate soldier, holding a Civil War style rifle musket. Betty thought they had caught a reenactor out exploring in the dark like they were. But this soldier knew the battlefield perhaps a little better than any reenactor could have.

Looking west toward Reynolds Woods.

Reenactors are trained never to aim a rifle at anyone, even in their counterfeit battles. Watch them. You will see them at the last minute, discreetly lift the muzzle a fraction just in case some foreign body happened to be in the barrel. This fellow whom they encountered in what was once purely Confederate held territory, suddenly brought the weapon down and aimed it at the two women. He said to Betty, "You don't belong here, Yank. Now, git!"

She turned to her daughter and said, "Look, let's leave. I don't know what's going on here, but...." And the soldier began to fade, and fade, and fade, until his visible presence upon this world and in this plane of reality was taken from him, just as it had been one hundred and thirty some years before.

Betty has been coming to Gettysburg for about four years. She says that she cannot go anywhere on the battlefield and not "hear" cannon fire. That started the first time she visited Gettysburg, and has increased ever since. She feels as if she has been to Gettysburg before—meaning in a previous life—a feeling many have who are drawn to the place.

Betty does not mind talking about the terminal illness she has. Slowly, in minor ways, it is affecting her brain. Her short term memory is failing, but her long term memory remains fine. One positive thing about this terrible illness is that during its course, her extra-sensory perception has increased, by her estimate, "about a hundred-fold." To Mollie on that hot summer night, she was about to prove it undeniably.

She was in an area adjacent to the "battlefield"—meaning private property near what the government owns. (Trust me, the soldiers did not stop fighting at the current National Park Service boundary lines, halt and say, "one day there will be a National Park Visitor Center right here, so let's stop making history on this spot and walk around these thirty acres and fight over there," as some would have us believe. The battlefield is everywhere.) There were some low bushes. Her first experience was that she smelled tobacco smoke; she looked around at everyone in the group, and no one was smoking, nor was there anyone near the tour group to provide the scent of burning tobacco.

The tour was over, and Betty stood waiting at the back of the group to talk with Mollie. Casually looking several yards away from the tour, she saw what she described as looking like a firefly glowing off in the grass. She finally reached Mollie, but was distracted by the light. Inexplicably, she had to go over to the grass to examine what was glowing there.

As she approached the spot, the light grew stronger and brighter, a luminescent gold color. When Betty got to the spot she realized that whatever was glowing was doing so from under the ground, beneath the earth, not just from the grass. By the time she got to it to pick it up, she said it was an area of light, about the size of a basketball. Mollie saw her bend down and pick something up. Betty knew as soon as she touched it, that it was meant for Mollie.

As Mollie remembered the event, Betty had come up to her, peered out into the darkened fields and said, "They're standing there all in a row." Mollie was apprehensive, of course. Suddenly Betty began walking out toward the field, stopped, and began working her fingers in the grass which had not been cut and was about ten inches high. Mollie thought that perhaps she had dropped something, and figuring she could help out with her lantern, asked Betty if she needed a light. Betty replied in the negative.

By now Betty had stood up and was walking toward Mollie. She dropped what Mollie thought was a rock into her hand. At first Mollie was unsure of what to say to a woman who had just given her a rock. But when she looked down into her hand, she saw that it was perfectly round. Closer examination showed that it was a button.

Mollie now was astounded. She knew that when the woman had walked the few feet from her and bent down, there was nothing in her open palms. For her to walk directly to a spot and pick up a manmade artifact from the ground, she must have been guided there.

Mollie told the woman that she was amazed, that she had never seen anything like that in all her years as a Civil War enthusiast, and that it was the thrill of the whole tour season for her to see something like that happen. She began to give the button back, when Betty took Mollie's hand, closed it around the button and said, "Oh, no, my dear. They want you to have it."

Mollie has taken it to two experts on antique buttons. Independently, they told her that it is a button from the Mexican War. Fought in the late 1840s, that war was a training ground for many West Point graduates who would later become Civil War officers, both for the Union and the Confederacy. The button has an eagle with the letter "I" embossed upon it. Confederates, at the beginning of the war, often wore older uniforms, or when buttons were lost, replaced them with older buttons from worn out uniforms. The experts identified it as a Confederate staff officer's button.

Of course, there have been instances of items disappearing in the presence of supernatural phenomena—moving, or removing items seems to be a hallmark of some mischievous spirits. More rarely is a physical item passed from the other dimension into this one. Even more rare is the instance where an item is passed into this world from the other, then, as if to make certain it is not missed, it is pointed out to one of us possessing that unique quality some call, "The Gift."

PAGEANT OF THE MACABRE

The muffled drum's sad roll has beat
The soldier's last tattoo
No more on life's parade shall meet
Those brave and fallen few.

Rest on embalmed and sainted dead
Dear as the blood ye gave
No impious footstep here shall tread
The herbage of your grave.
—Theodore O'Hara

In all of warfare over the millennia there can be nothing more terrifying than hand-to-hand combat. In battle it is one thing to lob a shell at what appears to be a group of ants two miles away, or to unleash a volley with five hundred other riflemen at a line of color that happens to be infantry at three hundred yards, or to drop a bomb from 35,000 feet. It is yet another thing entirely to see the desperate, dirt and sweat-stained face of a child-warrior coming rapidly toward you with perfect malice, with the business end of a bayonet or the ten-pound butt of a rifle aimed at your head. But more frightening is that at that moment it is the mirror image of yourself you see; and it is Death close-up into whose countenance you gaze.

Americans on both sides must have been reluctant to engage in hand-to-hand combat. Standard tactics of the Revolutionary War period dictated that soldiers in line fire a volley at about 50 to 75 yards—the effective range of the smooth-bore "Brown Bess,"—then sprint to the enemy with bayonets fixed hoping to break his line. The wounded were finished off with the particularly evil looking triangular bayonet. But in the Civil War, the frequency of bayonet wounds to other types of wounds was only one-tenth of one percent. Bayonets were used as candle holders far more often than as combat weapons.

When hand-to-hand combat occurred, it was savage. Descriptions of the close-in fighting during Longstreet's Assault (popularly known as "Pickett's Charge,") are rife with men clubbing each other over the head with the musket butt or heavy barrel, wrestling on the ground, or using rocks from the stone wall to crush each others' skulls. Perhaps what Confederate Col. William C. Oates saw during his fight for Little Round Top was the reason men were reluctant to utilize the "cold steel":

"A Maine man reached to grasp the staff of the colors when Ensign Archibald stepped back and Sergeant Pat O'Conner stove his bayonet through the head of the Yankee, who fell dead. I witnessed that incident, which impressed me beyond the point of being forgotten."[1] As it would any normal human being.[2]

As distasteful as hand-to-hand combat was to the Civil War soldier, it seems that, whenever there was a crisis point in a battle, it was earmarked by face-to-face, personal, one-on-one immolations.

All modern Civil War enthusiasts—like the original veterans of the great conflict—look for the proverbial "High Water Mark" of the war. The Battle of Antietam—because the South was never so close to British recognition—was the watershed, according to at least one historian. Yet a Confederate victory at Gettysburg, or even later, might have altered the thinking in Parliament; after all, Great Britain, throughout the war sold 400,000 of the prized Enfield rifle muskets to the U. S. government while selling an equal number to the Confederates!

Once the buffs have narrowed it enough, the majority usually comes to light upon Gettysburg as the watershed battle; and the climactic battle within the battle, to many, is Pickett's Charge on July 3, 1863.

But there were several "High Water Marks" at Gettysburg, in addition to the one on July 3. There were perhaps half a dozen or so moments when all could have been changed, and the world as we know it today, altered forever in inexplicable ways.

And while historians refer to Longstreet's Assault as a climax of the battle, others may also refer to the evening of July 1, when Confederate commander Robert E. Lee ordered his subordinate Lieutenant General Richard Ewell to attack Cemetery Hill, if practicable. For some reason, perfectly logical to Gen. Ewell then—and just as completely nonsensical to us now—he did not attack.

In fact, the sun was setting behind the South Mountain range over twenty-four hours later when Confederate General Early's men, having lain hidden on the reverse slope in front of Cemetery Hill, rose up and began their assault. It seems ironic now, and it may have seemed like some sort of "gallows humor" then, that 3,500 men of the South advanced, with their objective a cemetery.

Union artillery on Cemetery Hill immediately opened, but Early's men came on, driving a line of Federal infantry from the bottom of the hill. Then, after braving fire from a Maine battery to their left and rear, they overran and routed another line of Yankees, some of whom, in their haste to escape the Rebels, ran panic-stricken into the fire of their own artillery and were chewed up by canister.

In one of the artillery manuals published around the beginning of the war, the writer recommended that before going into battle, artillerists should be relieved of their personal weapons—the pistol and curved saber—and that they should be placed in the wagons and stored in the rear of the lines. The natural tendency of man, he explained, when rushed by attacking troops, is to abandon the cannon, which requires teamwork to fire, and rely upon his personal weapons to defend himself. That writer was John Gibbon, fighting at Gettysburg himself, just a few hundred yards west of Cemetery Hill. Soon there would be reason enough, had any of the Federal artillerists on Cemetery Hill read that section of the manual, to curse Gibbon with their dying breaths.

The Confederates rush the guns. Gunners pull the lanyards one last time but out through the great clouds of smoke come the surviving Confederates, screaming the Rebel yell for all they were worth. Handspikes—the club-like handle stuck in the trail that helped aim the cannon—swing with deadly heft like primitive baseball bats against skulls; rammers and even fence rails knock down Louisianians; rocks from the stone walls and clubbed muskets batter men's heads and faces into bloody pulp. Men shout and curse in Louisiana Cajun French and immigrant New York German. Almost miraculously, the cannoneers drive off the Confederates alone, without infantry support, in hand-to-hand combat.

Union foot soldiers finally arrive and finish the job driving the Rebels back down the hill. Had the Confederates succeeded in their assault, the Baltimore Pike—main retreat route for the Union Army at Gettysburg—would have been theirs; also, the rear of the Union line on Cemetery Hill, Cemetery Ridge and the Taneytown Road—another major retreat route—would have been open.

For all their effort, only two Confederates are known for sure to have held their position on Cemetery Hill. In fact they hold it still to this day, buried under several feet of Yankee clay, in Evergreen, Gettysburg's local cemetery.

For years, many of those who walked through the National Cemetery regularly would see a dark, cloaked figure moving—some claimed floating—through the grounds which had become the repository for the mortal remains of the heroes of Gettysburg, and other battles, who had given their lives, their futures, and, for some, even their very identities for the country they loved.

When he was described to historians, they nearly unanimously agreed that it was the uniform of a cavalry officer. When rangers went to chase the violator out of the consecrated grounds, the figure slipped on silent feet behind a tree. When the tree was circled by the investigating ranger, alas and to the ranger's extreme disappointment, no one was found.

Years passed. A mistake was found in the gravestones dotting the National Cemetery. A hero had been passed over. Captain William Miller, late of the 3rd Pennsylvania Cavalry, the only Medal of Honor winner from the Battle of Gettysburg known to be buried there, was not given the coveted gold gilt tombstone reserved for recipients of the nation's highest award. The change in headstones was made. The peripatetic vision of the dark cavalryman has been seen no more.[3]

And while one restless spirit seems to have found eternal rest, others have replaced him in the quest for what is precious to one from beyond the grave's wide and ultimate maw.

Since June 1994, *The Ghosts of Gettysburg Candlelight Walking Tours®* has been entertaining visitors to Gettysburg with tales of the paranormal during the evening hours. Being a guide for the tours seems to place one in a unique position with the entities from the Other World. Many of our guides have had paranormal experiences of their own.

One of our guides told me of a night during the 1999 season when she was standing at the low stone wall just to the north of where the immovable men of Battery I, 1st New York Light Artillery, swatted with fence rails and rammers at men armed with lethal muskets. She noticed that some of her customers were looking beyond her, into the darkened field of conflict over the wall. As she said, she thought she was "losing them," that she wasn't telling the story in an interesting enough manner. Finally, the story ended, and as she was about to suggest they move on to the next stop, those who had been distracted finally spoke up.

"Look! You can still see it," they said excitedly. "Have you ever had this happen before?"

She turned just in time to see a tall blue column just over the New Yorkers' position begin to fade into the darkness of the deserted killing field.

"Your tours don't provide special effects, do they?" asked one of her people

Awestruck herself at what she just witnessed, she assured them that *Ghosts Gettysburg Candlelight Walking Tours*® does not supply special effects for their tours, and especially not on National Park Service property where, as commercial venture, they are forbidden to go.

The blue light makes sense: it is one of the colors frequently associated with sightings of paranormal entities. But why at that moment? No one knows for sure I'd like to think it was the storyteller herself, weaving a particularly entrancing tale that encouraged the blue spirit energy to participate in its own story.

Interestingly enough, while doing research for this book, I ran across a letter dated May 25, 1997, from one of our former guides who has gone on to do research and teach in the field of parapsychology. She recounted a tour that she was leading to the same spot on Cemetery Hill. This particular night was very dark. There was no moon. Nothing could be seen on the hill, not even the outlines of the monuments. Even though it was pitch black, as she wrote, "the Hancock statue was lit up with a strange blue light which seemed to come from within the statue itself."

She felt it strange that only this one statue was illuminated by the unearthly light and none of the others. Casting about, as we all do when confronted with the impossible, she rationalized that perhaps it was a reflection from the High School stadium lights. Yet the other equestrian statue—that of Union general O. O. Howard—had no light on it, nor did any of the half dozen battery and regimental markers. And, as we in Gettysburg know, the lights coming from the stadium are a brilliant white, not blue.

Our guide and her group continued to stare at the bizarre blue light emanating from within the cold bronze statue. But she was under a time constraint to get her group back to headquarters by a certain hour, and so directed them to return toward the Jennie Wade House. As she did so, a couple from the group ap proached her and asked if she had seen what happened after they began to leave the site. She said no, and they proceeded to tell her that, as she turned and began to walk down Cemetery Hill, the blue light suddenly extinguished. Looking toward the high school, she realized that the lights from the stadium had not changed, again eliminating that possibility. "Mark," she wrote, "I feel sure that something of a paranormal nature took place that night. I now wish I could have walked over to the statue to investigate it...I never saw it so pitch black like that before on the hill. And that blue light. It just seemed to pulsate from within the statue itself. I remember thinking that the color of it put me in mind of the same color as the Blue Boy."[4]

It was another misty, rainy May evening, about 8:45. There were only three couples on one of our Baltimore Street tours and one of our veteran guides had just told them the stories at the wall on the north side of East Cemetery Hill. In the shadowy distance loomed the statue of O. O. Howard, and the dark mass of Culp's Hill. She had just finished her last story. From the foggy heights of Culp's Hill, across the valley between Steven's Knoll and East Cemetery Hill, and up the slope of Cemetery Hill came a low, building sound. It caught the attention of the guide and her customers. They turned to listen. What they heard was impossible, but undeniable. It was the hoarse roar from thousands of throats, like men preparing for victory or preparing for their confrontation with their Maker.

Confusion crossed the faces of the customers. "What's over that way?" asked one. "Culp's Hill," answered the guide. "Is there a football game going on?" he asked again. "Not in May," she replied. "Besides, the stadium is that way," a good ninety degrees to the left of their line to the sounds on Culp's Hill. Then, they heard something even more bizarre.

From the mist-laden, black woods in the distance came a volley of musketry. Then the booming of cannon and more rifle fire. And once again, the husky mingling of shouts, hurrahs, and cheers. Then silence.

Aldous Huxley once wrote a small book about expanding the human mind using synthetic means. He called it, *The Doors of Perception*. Here, at Gettysburg, the doors of perception into another world open and close randomly and seemingly at their own whim. It is the fortunate who are prepared for, and accepting of, these rare glimpses into the world that awaits us all.

MASTERS OF THE RUINS

The distance that the dead have gone
Does not at first appear—
Their coming back seems possible
For many an ardent year.
　　　　　　　—Emily Dickinson

Gettysburg has an almost mystical attraction to many people, a pull that is unexplainable, in most cases. Siren-like, it draws millions from their comfortable homes hundreds or thousands of miles away, to a place where horror was master and king for three days of American tragedy. It is as if we are still ruled by our long dead fathers.

There is always the explanation that humans like to see the scene of a tragedy. Like modern day "rubberneckers" risking a car crash themselves to look at an auto accident in the other lane, in July 1863, people came from miles away to see where a huge battle took place. These were the first tourists to Gettysburg, bereaved and fearful relatives of soldiers who were in the battle and who, for some reason, had not been heard from since the fighting. Locals connected with them and took them to various sites on the field—the hill that took on the name of the Culp family; the two round-topped hills far to the south of town, one big, the other little; the spring once owned by the Spangler family; and the place locals had already dubbed with the eerie name of Devil's Den. Of course, the locals charged the mourners money for their escort service. Thus were born the battlefield guides, seen about the battlefield today, again and anon, ushering the unknowing into the hell-like horrors that were once Gettysburg.

The area between Little Round Top and Hauck's Ridge was given the Biblical sounding name of "The Valley of Death" either by the men who fought there or by locals. It is only a couple of hundred yards wide, and about a quarter mile long. Through it winds lazy Plum Run, rechristened "Bloody Run," because for a few hours in American history it literally ran red with the blood of the men who fought and fell beside it, and those who crawled to it in the blazing sun of July 2, 1863, for a last drink of water.

It was a natural sluiceway down which Confederates could have poured from Devil's Den. The fighting there held them, at least for awhile. A wise decision by Captain James E. Smith, commanding the 4th New York Artillery, divided his six guns. Four of them remained at the top of Devil's Den covering the Triangular Field; the other two he placed about a hundred yards behind and to his left, positioned to fire canister bounding down the valley should Confederates make it through the Den.

mith fought his four guns at the top of Devil's Den until his own infantry advanced in front of them. He retired to his section in what he called the "gully," the Valley of Death, begging tearfully with the remaining infantry to save his guns. It was not to be. A Confederate was seen astride one of the guns, waving the Rebel flag until he was knocked off by a gunner. Smith's guns atop Devil's Den were soon overrun and Confederates came pouring, like molten lead, into the Valley of Death.

Fortunately Smith himself had rushed to his remaining two guns sitting beside the ridge behind Devil's Den. He opened fire across the front of the onrushing Confederates with canister. Smith saw the Rebel flag fall and rise again three times before the Rebels were finally driven from the "gully."[1]

As the sun began to set behind the South Mountain range, tinting the sky to match the crimson valley below, the final moment of glory was saved for the Pennsylvania Reserves.

In war, fighting on your own soil is a nearly holy endeavor. Men will fight with a particular fanaticism, bordering on the suicidal, if they feel their homes and families are threatened. We saw it in Vietnam, in Korea, in the Soviet Union in World War II. Who knows how much the American Civil War would have been shortened if most of it had not been fought on Southern ground. By late afternoon of July 2, it was the Pennsylvanians' turn.

The two brigades of Pennsylvania Reserves made up Crawford's Division entirely. Some of the men had been plucked out of building the defenses of Washington, work given to the invalids. They were men who had already proved their mettle by being wounded before, had recovered enough to do some stationary work, but not enough for the rigors of a full campaign. As the Rebels entered Pennsylvania, however, the rules were abandoned and the men exchanged shovels and picks for rifles and bayonets.

One brigade of the Reserves advanced from behind Little Round Top and planted themselves on the northern summit. For about 20 minutes they calmly watched the fighting slowly rolling toward them. Then they watched as fragments of units—unarmed men, stragglers, and clots of soldiers—tumbled back across Plum Run, the little stream running through the valley. Close behind the refugees were the Confederates on a straight course for Little Round Top.

General Crawford himself takes the colors. In the growing twilight the Reserves fire two volleys and charge headlong down the slope and into the massed Rebels. Sheer momentum drives the Confederates back to the blood-stained wheatfield.

It was through the Valley of Death where lights were first seen moving on the night of July 2, 1863. The yellowish candle-glow, meandering and stopping, lowering to the ground to illuminate a face twisted in a death agony, or one still animated with life to be carried off the field to the more horrible, makeshift operating tables.

A letter sent to me in 1994 recounted the strange experience of a husband and wife as they gazed from the summit of Little Round Top into the valley below. It was an October evening, about 8:00 p.m. The night was cool and clear. As they stood by the 91st Pennsylvania Monument, they looked to the left, into the darkened woods on the lower slope of Big Round Top at the southern end of the Valley of Death. The husband saw them first: an uneven row of four lights looking, as the woman put it, "like candles glowing."

They watched the mysterious glowing lights for approximately one minute when a car approached, heading toward the lights. The car stopped and parked, as if the driver and passengers had also seen the glow.

Anyone living in and around Gettysburg will tell you that, with the abundance of deer in the vicinity, eyes glowing whitish-yellow in the direct beams of automobile headlights are commonplace. But then, according to their letter, something unusual happened. The driver turned off his headlamps...and the four candle-like lights continued to glow.

Something else was amiss. Deer eyes caught in headlights always come in pairs. The woman drew a diagram to accompany her letter—the lights were single and spaced and staggered.

Thirty seconds passed and suddenly two of the lights dimmed and disappeared. Ten more seconds went by and another extinguished. The last light burned for only three more seconds, when it too died.

At first the woman thought it might have been a farmhouse in the woods, but she could not recall seeing one there while driving to Little Round Top. Indeed, there was never a farm established on the sloped side of Big Round Top or in the swampy Slaughter Pen at the southern end of the valley.

The couple was indeed mystified until they returned home with a copy of *Ghosts of Gettysburg*. Reading the book in bed one night, the wife came across the chapter entitled "Black Sunset." Therein I recount a few of the sightings of phantom campfires and dots of luminescence seen in various sites from the battlefield to the South Mountain passes from whence the Confederate Army debouched to do the worst thing living men can do to one another. A chill went through her and her hair stood on end. She woke her husband to read him the paragraph. He agreed that it was very strange.

They might have been even more amazed had they read the account in *More Ghosts of Gettysburg*, of the young man watching, one night, from Little Round Top, some spectral lights floating above the floor of the Valley of Death, stopping then moving on...then stopping....

Or, if they had had the opportunity to read a letter I received from a man recalling his experience from the summit of Little Round Top around 1990. Being reenactors, he and his family had visited Gettysburg numerous times in the past, sometimes several times a year. But this particular year was to present the gentleman with a completely new appreciation for the battlefield.

It was twilight, probably more toward dark since he remembered that all the tourists had finally left. Leaving his family in the car in the lot just below the summit, he found a spot at the crest overlooking the fabled Valley of Death. He was alone. It was July 2, anniversary of the great bloodletting on that part of the battlefield.

The sun had already set, no doubt the reason for the tourists' exodus from the hill. Perhaps his mind wandered a little, in an attempt to try and imagine just what it must have been like in the valley, that seething cauldron of fear and death, that once boiled below him. Suddenly, just to the right of Devil's Den, he saw a flash of light. At first, he thought it came from a passing car, or was perhaps an odd reflection. Indeed, there is a road that winds behind the woods to the north of Devil's Den and paths meander through that area. But, he realized, there were no cars there.

Another flash caught his eye, this time to the left of Devil's Den. Then another, again to the right, then several amongst the rocks of the Den itself. His description was that it looked like a bunch of people with flash cameras had spread out and were taking pictures of Little Round Top, almost as if they had been organized to do so.

Another oddity was that the flashes were not white, like camera flashes, but bright yellow. His first thoughts were to seek a logical answer to the lights: fireflies, car lights, the moon, all were rapidly dismissed. It finally dawned on him that the flashes he had seen looked like muskets being fired from the rocks of Devil's Den. The "firing" went on for at least a minute as he sat spellbound by the sight.

His daughter arrived on Little Round Top to see if he was ready to leave, since it was dark. He asked her to look down into the valley and tell him what she saw. She said she could not see much because of the darkness. He looked at her and she was looking out to the right. When he turned back to look at the Den, as if ordered by some long-dead commander, the "firing" had ceased.

He wrote that he spent a lot of time looking for a logical explanation as to what he witnessed that night from Little Round Top, but all logical answers elude him. "I believe and will always believe that I saw the flash of muskets being fired up at Little Round Top. I have never had a better understanding of what happened there in July of 1863."

MYSTERIES OF OAK RIDGE

Just death, kind umpire of men's miseries.
—Henry VI, Act I, scene ii

On McPherson's Ridge to the west of Gettysburg, the Southern brigades of Archer and Davis lined up shoulder-to-shoulder and advanced toward Gettysburg straddling the Cashtown Road. They ran into the dismounted cavalry of Brig. Gen. John Buford which held them long enough for Maj. Gen. John F. Reynolds and his Federal 1st Corps to arrive on the field. Reynolds, of course, was riding to meet a Confederate bullet, still in some Rebel's cartridge box for another fifteen minutes or so.

As more and more units marched to the sound of the guns on the morning of July 1, 1863, the lines stretched farther north, along Oak Ridge to Oak Hill. The fighting was fierce along Oak Ridge, from the railroad cut on the south to the Mummasburg Road to the north. Iverson's Confederate Brigade, because of a tactical foul-up, was annihilated in one long, neat row as if they were still marching into battle. On certain nights, witnesses say, you can still hear the noises they made as they marched into the palm of Death's grizzled hand and he closed his fist: the men moan and cry out, shout orders and curses, and hundreds of Yankee bullets thud into bodies, finding their mark.

Farther down the line stood the men of the 11th Pennsylvania. With them was their little mascot, Sallie "the War Dog," who, when the rest of the regiment was forced to retreat, stayed faithfully behind without food or water for three days, snapping at strangers in gray or blue, ferociously guarding the dead of her regiment until their comrades returned to bury them. She is still there today, nobly resting on the west side of the monument, crafted in bronze as directed by the survivors, guarding now only the spirits of the men whose earthly forms she once so fiercely protected.

War mascots have always been a part of man's belligerent endeavors. There was "Old Abe" the war eagle of the 8th Wisconsin during the Civil War, and "Willie," George S. Patton's dog whose lack of courage got his name changed from "William the Conqueror." There is no doubt that the dog mascots loved their masters—a whole regiment of them—with a love that humans can only hope to understand one day.

Union Brig. Gen. Thomas L. Kane was given a lesson on the fealty of the canine to its often unworthy masters at Gettysburg:

A pet dog belonging to a company of the 1st Maryland (Confederate) charged with the Reg't, ran ahead of them when their progress was arrested, & came in among the Boys in Blue as if he supposed they were what in better days they might have been—merely the men of another noisy hose or engine company, competing for precedence with his masters, in the smoke of a burning building. At first, some of my men said, he barked in valorous glee; but I myself first saw him on three legs going between our own men & the Men in Gray on the ground as though looking for a dead master, or seeking on which side he might find an explanation of the tragedy he witnessed, intelligible to his canine apprehension. He licked someone's hand, they said, after he was perfectly riddled. Regarding him as the only Christian-minded being on either side, I ordered him to be honorably buried.[1]

Then there was the "last stand" of the boys of the 16th Maine, who were told, like some other Maine boys at the opposite end of the line, to "hold their position at all costs." But this order was a little different from that given their comrades from the 20th Maine at Little Round Top the next day: the rest of the army was leaving them behind, not coming toward them. They were to be the rear guard for the retreat.

They were sent to where the Mummasburg Road crests, then descends Oak Ridge, and were given the fateful order to hold it at all costs. Little did they know that it was that point where two Confederate wings, like two huge blades of the same set of sharpened shears, would come together. By one account, of the 275 men standing on Oak Ridge in the afternoon of July 1, only 43 would make it back to Cemetery Ridge by night.[2]

Their monument stands on the Mummasburg Road. Veterans of the units always liked to place their monuments at the most advanced point of action, where they were closest to the enemy. In this case, the location of the monument is a little misleading. The Mainers were pushed from that spot by overwhelming numbers of Rebels; indeed it was the farthest advance toward the enemy they made that day, but it was not the closest they would get to them.

Slowly they were pushed back along Oak Ridge, resisting fiercely as best they could, until they reached the cut in the earth made for the future railroad line. It seemed for a moment as if they were sinking into the earth, for they were indeed descending below ground level. For all, it was a premonition of the future that eventually comes to all men; to some in the 16th, the future would come a little sooner than for others. Moments after they found refuge in the earth, the Rebels found them.[3]

As they were overrun in the easternmost railroad cut by the Rebels demanding they surrender their flag, they ripped it from its staff, and tore it to bits. They hid the fragments of bars and stars in their clothes, to go to prison with them or, in many cases, to prison graveyards at Andersonville, or Libby, or Belle Isle, where the pieces lie yet today, moldering along with the heroes who bore them there.

Years after the war, in response to a toast to "Gettysburg," General Joshua L. Chamberlain addressed the survivors of the 16th Maine. The ghosts—living and dead—from those prison graveyards arose and gathered. Near the end of the speech, referring to how he had heard that they had "lost" their colors, he brought them cheering to their feet, magnificent orator that he was. But cheers turned to solemn tears when one of the old veterans reached into his vest pocket and pulled out a tattered and stained star, a relic from that glorious day when honor meant more than life, which he had carried all those years. Chamberlain continued: "Lost? There is a way of losing that is finding. When soul overmasters sense; when the noble and divine self overcomes the lower self; when duty and honor and love,—immortal things,—bid the mortal perish! It is only when a man supremely gives that he supremely finds. That was your sacrifice; that is your reward."

And so it is to this ridge named after the tree that grows upon it, once watered by the blood of patriots and heroes, that people still come. As if the men who fought there still send out solemn reminders of their sacrifice, strange, unexplainable events still occur to visitors to Oak Ridge.

Take, for example, the man exploring Oak Ridge in 1991. The sun was just setting behind the South Mountains to the west. Anyone who has been there at dusk can empathize with the employees of farmer Forney, who owned the parcel of land just to the west, where there was planted, for a number of years after the battle, several hundred of Iverson's North Carolinians. Instead of the corn or wheat sown in the field that spring, the farmhands ended up reaping the spirits of Iverson's men, who rose like some unwanted and hideous crop, to terrorize them.

The man walked past the monument to the men of the 11th Pennsylvania and its brave little mascot Sallie. He had gotten about 100 yards out, probably passing the site of Iverson's men's burial, when he became the recipient of a rare gift from the battlefield. Looking down, he spotted what looked like a cannonball. He stooped to touch it. Sure enough, it was not smooth rock, but cool symmetrical iron that met his fingers. Since he was "exploring" he decided to continue his walk. But after just a couple of steps, he stopped and realized what a rare find he had stumbled across, and turned to retrieve it.

Although he had walked only a step or two from it, when he returned to the spot, it was gone. Certainly it was the right spot, for there, beneath his fingers, was the depression where the rare projectile had been. Certainly he was alone in that once terrible field where cannonballs like the one he had seen and touched were scythes of death and destruction. He searched the area for another 45 minutes, but for no use: the agent of death, like the men it had sent on their one-way journey, had been removed from the earth in an instant.

Two years later, he returned to Gettysburg and related the story to a battle-field guide. You can imagine how both were astounded when the guide related that exactly seven days before his encounter with the phantom artillery shell, two men had told the guide that they had seen a cannonball in that very field, and when they returned for it, it too had disappeared, leaving only an indentation and a mystery where once solid iron had lain.

11th Pennsylvania monument on Doubleday Avenue.

Perhaps it is lying there right now, waiting for another unsuspecting soul to find it, then lose it again to the unknown.

The Doubleday Inn is one of the more delightful and well-placed bed and breakfasts in Gettysburg. It sits on Oak Ridge and overlooks the Gettysburg College campus and the town beyond. Doubleday Avenue, where the Inn is located, winds around in a fairly large loop as it changes its name to Wadsworth Avenue, past the Union Cavalry line markers on Buford Avenue, and the site of the old Forney Farm, then past the Peace Light Memorial on North Confederate Avenue, until it returns to the Inn. It is a nice walk...most of the time.

For one couple, the first week in May seems to hold a special place in the spirit world of Gettysburg.

Being from Massachusetts, they naturally wanted to visit the site where some of the men from their state had battled on Oak Ridge. The 12th Massachusetts fought near the Mummasburg Road. In fact, when O'Neal's entire Confederate Brigade attacked that end of the line, the 12th, along with the 90th Pennsylvania and two other regiments, swung to the right and delivered a volley of fire that sent O'Neal's men tumbling back, thus setting up the solitary destruction of Iverson's Brigade a few minutes later. The couple ventured to the 12th Massachusetts monument. As they approached the monument they were overtaken by a distinct drop in temperature.

It was not the first time this had happened. They had visited the monument a number of times before, and, sure enough, the temperature had dropped each time they approached the spot. Ominously, their letter to me states, "Even during the day things seem colder there, but at night even more happens."

Their first experience was in 1994. It was a quiet May night as they walked to the 12th Massachusetts monument. Still and calm, the battlefield—and especially the area of Iverson's Pits—holds surprises that we of this world are unaware of.

As she put it, they decided to "tempt fate," and walked behind the monument, over the low stone wall, and out into the darkened fields where over 500 North Carolina boys poured out their life's blood into the Yankee loam. They stopped. Suddenly, she felt something strike the arch on the right side of her right foot. She looked down to see what it was. She could not have walked into anything since she had been standing still and there was nothing near her foot but packed earth. It could not have been her husband; he was on her left. Still she asked, "Did you just touch my foot?" He replied in the negative, but told her that he had just felt an icy coldness in the shape of a Christian cross, pressed against his spine.

Events which have no obvious genesis visible in this world are frightening. And so they left the darkened fields which were sanctified by the sacrifice of the North Carolinians.

Sometimes we just cannot stay away from what we cannot explain. Paranormal experiences, frightening though they may be, fascinate humans probably because we want to go to the edge of life, to the very brink, of heaven...or hell. So, two years later, once again in May, they returned to Gettysburg. This time they stayed at the Doubleday Inn, purposely to be able to visit the spot near the Massachusetts monument again.

Visit it they did—four times during that trip, each when the veil of night covered the once grisly field of fighting. Two of the nights were blustery; two were as still as a tomb. They ventured over the wall on one of the quiet nights. As they began to walk tentatively out toward the temporary sepulcher of the North Carolinians, in the distance to their right, from the same direction Iverson's doomed men advanced, quietly at first, then gradually getting louder, they heard a rustling in the brush like someone was moving toward them. They left for that night, but courageously returned three more times during their stay.

On the two blustery nights, they heard nothing. They ran through the possibilities: animals, or possibly more wind than they originally thought. But the last night they visited, they took note that wind conditions were very still, the same as they remembered from the first night they had heard the noises.

As they carefully trod the earth where heroes once bled, the noises started again, as if some unseen soul (or a whole regiment of souls) was advancing toward them from their right flank. This second time they noticed that there were more noises than the first time, a whole brigade of noises mustering in the dark. The other thing they noticed was that the closer they got to the site of Iverson's Pits, the more noises they heard moving toward them.

Do they see us? Do the dead watch us from Beyond? There are times when they seem to care about us, even protect us, at least those of us they loved in this life. Or are they merely curious about who is intruding upon their quiet, peaceful, eternal rest?

In their letter, they said they never believed in ghosts before. But there is something about Gettysburg that makes believers out of some of the most avid skeptics.

I received a letter in 1995 from a former Seminarian to whom I had spoken concerning an experience several of his party had on Oak Ridge. In October 1994 he, his wife, and four other friends were touring the battlefield using the tour tape, traveling south on Doubleday Avenue. It was a beautiful, sunny day. They were somewhere past the observation tower when one of their group said, "Look who's coming."

A Union officer on horseback passed them, galloping close enough so they might see his epaulets, and they could identify him as a captain. They said they saw him riding southward to the "white house"—which I assume was the Doubleday Inn or perhaps another house on that side of the avenue—dismount, and enter quickly as if he were on some mission. Thinking there might be an encampment nearby and wishing to garner some information from the reenactor, they drove quickly to the house, consuming far less than a minute from the time they saw him enter and the time they pulled up in front of the house.

I personally have seen a mounted man ride to the Doubleday Inn. For what reason, I do not know. He may have been a reenactor-friend of the former owners, stopping by for a cold glass of water. I do know, however, that whoever he was, he rode in the hoofprints of scores of young aides and adjutants and couriers, riding rapidly from regimental commanders to brigade commanders to division commanders, who had temporary "field headquarters"—no tents, but simply their aides gathered around and their personal flag—along that side of the ridge. The couriers carried vital, battle-altering orders. Some made it to deliver their messages, some did not.

But for the observers of the captain, by the time they got to the white house, there was no sign of the rider, or his horse. All in the car saw him ride to and arrive at his destination. Not a single one of the six people in the car saw him leave.

Of course, there is always the chance that the horseman they saw was indeed a reenactor who somehow departed without being seen. Common sense would certainly dictate that. Except for a letter I received in 1997.

The subject of the letter was Sallie, the mascot of the 11th Pennsylvania. The couple that wrote found themselves tremendously moved by the little terrier who returned the offering of food scraps, clean water, and some straw to sleep on with a loyalty that bade her to starve to death rather than yield the bodies of her dead but still beloved masters to strangers.

The woman, being an animal lover, proposed to place a dog biscuit as a symbol on little Sallie's memorial. It was not a planned thing; she had always wanted to do it; they were right there, and even though it was night, being from Tennessee, who knew when they would make it back. They stopped their vehicle, actually had to back up since it was such a spur-of-the-moment thing, and parked at the monument. The lady got out of the truck and sorted through the stuff behind the seat until she pulled a biscuit from the box of them she keeps for her neighbor's dog. Just as she found the biscuit, she looked at her husband and said, "Did you hear anything?"

"No," he said. "What did it sound like?" He looked through the rear window onto the moonlit road and battlefields beyond, but saw nothing.

"I heard a boot or shoe scuff on the pavement." He had heard nothing but the noise from her search for the biscuit. She turned slowly to walk behind the truck, but suddenly jumped, and gasped, "Oh, my God!"

"What's the matter?"

"I felt someone standing right here, close enough to put my hand on their chest!" Her husband looked, but there was no one there. He paused and thought for a moment, as anyone might—was it time to get out of there?

"Is there any feeling of negativity—coldness or anything like that?" he asked.

"No," she replied, "but I feel they're just curious about what we're doing here."

"Well, go ahead and put the biscuit on the monument so they'll know we mean no harm or disrespect."

She walked quickly around the truck and the monument, placed the biscuit before the beloved bronze replica of the little dog, and returned to the vehicle. She said she felt the eerie presence had departed, apparently happy with their intentions. They summed it up best in their letter: "As we drove slowly on down Oak Ridge, we decided that as Sallie had watched over the men of the 11th who fell in battle, perhaps they were guarding her memorial in return. We had apparently encountered one of Sallie's soldiers on spectral sentry duty, patrolling the hallowed ground where they fought and fell...."

And while the main story of their letter counts as one of the ghostly experiences so common on the Gettysburg Battlefield, something they wrote in the beginning of the letter is important to the former Seminarian and his friends who saw the young captain riding the lines.

Explaining why they were driving past the monument to the 11th Pennsylvania, the husband mentioned that, after taking one of our ghost tours, they wanted to check out the Peace Light Memorial. The reason was because, many years ago, his wife had seen something completely divorced from logic or reason out there on Oak Hill and the ridge that extends from it.

From behind the Peace Light, she had seen the ghostly figure of a horse and rider appear, ride from left to right as if he were about to head south down Oak Ridge, then vanish before her eyes. Could he have been the same young officer seen by the others? Skepticism is such a darn hard thing to keep...at Gettysburg!

But perhaps the most bizarre occurrence to date in the area of Oak Ridge was documented in a letter dated February 2, 1996. There was a cover letter by a mother who had once stayed at the Doubleday Inn with her two grown daughters. It was about 10:30 that cold winter night when they ventured from the warm, comfortable confines of the Inn into what may have been a temporary lifting of the veil of time.

The two sisters decided they would take a nice walk in the freshly-fallen snow. Leaving the Inn they turned left, then began to curve around to the right as Doubleday Avenue becomes Wadsworth. It was indeed a lovely, snow-covered night, far in time and mood from those sultry, hot days of July 1863, when the ridge along which they walked held sweaty, fear-filled young men and boys bent upon breaking the Fifth Commandment with a vengeance, then to suffer for the rest of their lives—whether that be three score years or three score seconds—for their misdeed. A little past the marker for the 95th New York Infantry, they began to hear it.

At first they thought it sounded like a group of people sitting around in the woods having a party. They stopped to listen, and the chatter stopped. They started to walk again and it began again. Every time they stopped, the noise stopped.[4]

They are so maddeningly elusive, these spirits, these entities. They must know so much. Why don't they just show themselves, or speak up? Oh, the questions we could ask, of the battle they suffered through, of their migrations since, and of their pilgrimage back to the place where they left this plane of existence. Do they not answer because they are teasing us, because they do not want to answer our silly questions...or is it because they cannot....

Then, from the cold, darkened woods, a strange echo from the past. A song. They stopped to listen, and the song stopped. They began to walk again, and the chatter began anew.

One of the women suddenly decided she needed to get closer to the sound, and, uninvited, began to walk into the woods. Her sister felt as if she were already close enough to this private party, whether taking place in this world or the next, but she certainly did not want to stand in the dark on that once embattled ridge by herself. So she entered the woods too.

As the woods slowly closed around them, once again the conversation began, but it seemed that the closer they got to the sound, the farther away it moved, always staying the same distance from them. Still they could not see anyone associated with the noises.

Nowhere in any published works that I know of is that piece of woods identified as a field hospital. It is the area across which the 76th New York and 56th Pennsylvania retreated after being attacked by Mississippians and North Carolinians. And, of course, it is where the 95th New York fought. Yet men were wounded all over that area, and during the heat of battle were often taken temporarily to the shelter of nearby woods, for its shade. I checked the old maps. Yes, there were woods and shade for the wounded in that same area where they are today. Sometimes a surgeon would check in to these temporary sites, and quickly treat the more seriously wounded. Amputations in that situation were probably rare, but the gathering together of the hideously wounded for transport to a field hospital—like the house of John Forney just to the rear of these woods—would no doubt occur. But lifting and carrying the grievously wounded was so painful for them....

The letter-writer tells it best: "Then we started hearing things I particularly could have done without hearing. There was an agonizing scream. Then a lot of sobbing. Out of the muffled conversation there was one voice that stood out above the rest. This voice then yelled, 'Get up, get up, Go! Go!'"

They continued to walk, albeit a little more cautiously, until they were about fifteen or twenty feet into the woods, but still could not see any living soul.

"The sobbing and horrible screams continued," she wrote. "Then we heard 'Charge!' Both of us looked at each other to confirm what we had heard."

Apparently the one sister felt that there were people back in the trees and thickets on this February night, in the snowy woods, having a weird party, for she picked up the pace, heading deeper and deeper into the woods.

They heard metal rattling. She likened it to the sound a belt buckle would make if you shook it—or perhaps the metal pieces of a horse harness.

They came upon a thinned-out section of the woods with a large rock in the center of it. They stood motionless. Suddenly they heard a sound she described as a loud "crack!" They looked to their right from where the report had come, but again saw nothing. And now, it seems, they had entered into a different realm of the supernatural, where noises were changing to a visual confirmation of the Other World. The area in which they were standing, and that immediate area only, she emphasized, began to glow and become illuminated with that odd blue light which so many times before has presaged some imminent supernatural event.

Her sister wanted to continue on her quest into the unknown, which seemed to be unfolding before their eyes and in their presence, but suddenly the author of the letter began to get an intense feeling of sadness, and began to weep and shake uncontrollably. She was afraid the events they were hearing were about to become events that could be seen.

"All I kept telling her was that I didn't want to see what accompanied these horrible sounds. I didn't want to see them dying."

Her sister gave in and they ran through the woods and into a field, then made their way back to Wadsworth Avenue. At that moment a red pickup truck zoomed by, fishtailing in the snow.

So, you think. Now we know the source for the weird noises, and the party sounds, and the mock sobbing and horrible screams and the counterfeit orders to "get up!" and "Charge!" It was simply a truckload of local kids having fun on a snowy winter's night. And now they have left. That explains it all....

They started walking back to the Inn, feeling perhaps a little more at ease having seen the red truck fly by, and realizing that there just might be a rational explanation for what they heard.

They reached the woods again...and there it was...again! Softly emanating from the bare trees, sounds like low conversation came to their ears. They quickened their pace, and held hands from fear, like they were kids again. They reached the Inn, found their mother and related the story that put the lie to reason and logic. The letter writer could not talk to her mother about the horrible cries and screams, the sobbing, the orders to move to battle, without weeping.

They begged their mother to go back with them, to be certain that they had not been hallucinating. They put the video camera in the car, believing they would have the presence of mind to tape the horrid sounds or the otherworldly blue light. The writer promised to stay in the car with her mother while the other sister would go out and tape...whatever it was.

They parked the car on the side of the snow covered road. She got out of the car and entered the woods. No sooner had she stepped foot into the woods than the mother heard the shrill, agonized scream. Horrified at the sound, she covered her ears, uncontrollably curled up into a ball, welled up with tears and pleaded to leave. Her daughter screamed for her sister to get back into the car and they tore off.

For some reason, the sisters did not hear the terrible scream of pain that frightened their mother so badly. But when they asked their mother to vocalize what she had heard, it was the exact sound they had heard just minutes before, when they had entered those weird woods.

The ancient Egyptians, who have always seemed a little more open, a little more wise, or at least a little more accepting of death and the realization of an afterlife, played a favorite a board game called "Senet." It was a game based upon the players' adventures in the afterlife, and although Egyptian in origin, it seems it would be universal in theme and action and popular in any culture that will face its own inevitable conclusion. I shall always wonder who inspired the genesis of this game: was it some one living, or one of the dead come back....

And at Gettysburg, we seem to be always playing that game against opponents who know the rules better than we.

ENDNOTES

Mad Carnival
1. Though some historians consider this story apocryphal, it is found in Oliver Willcox Norton's *The Attack and Defense of Little Round Top*, for years a standard source for the fighting there.
2. William C. Oates, *The War Between the Union and the Confederacy and its Lost Opportunities*, New York: The Neale Publishing Company, 1905.
3. Thomas A. Desjardin, *Stand Firm Ye Boys From Maine*, Gettysburg, PA: Thomas Publications, 1995.
4. Oates, 219-227.

Dying Game
1. Andrew Brown, *Geology and the Gettysburg Campaign*, Commonwealth of Pennsylvania: 1962.
2. Garry E. Adelman and Timothy H. Smith have produced, in my opinion, the best history of the action in and around Devil's Den. *Devil's Den: A History and Guide*, Gettysburg, PA: Thomas Publications, 1997, is recommended reading for anyone interested in the actions there.
3. Mark Nesbitt, *35 Days to Gettysburg: The Campaign Diaries of Two American Enemies*, Stackpole Books, Harrisburg, PA, 1992.

Eden Afire
1. In 1976, the National Cemetery was considered "closed" to any new burials. Exceptions are wives and one dependent child of a veteran already interred in the Cemetery. As of September 1976, the total acreage, including the Annex on Steinwehr Avenue was 20.55. However, Civil War burials in one common grave continue as bodies continue to be found.

Climbing to Golgotha
1. Glenn Tucker, *High Tide at Gettysburg*, Bobbs-Merrill Co., Inc., New York: 1958, 300.
2. For a detailed account of the fighting on Culp's Hill, see Tucker, *High Tide at Gettysburg*, 304-305 and Edwin Coddington's *Gettysburg: A Study in Command*, Charles Scribner's Sons, New York, 1968.

Pageant of the Macabre
1. William C. Oates, 219.
2. Thomas A. Desjardin, in the appendix to his book, *Stand Firm Ye Boys From Maine*, does not mention any soldier from the unit killed by a bayonet to the head. There are, however, a number of men listed simply as "killed" among whom this unfortunate Maine man may be listed.
3. Mark Nesbitt, *Ghosts of Gettysburg*, Gettysburg, PA: Thomas Publications, 1991.
4. See *Ghosts of Gettysburg*.

Masters of the Ruins

1. Adelman and Smith, *Devil's Den*, Gettysburg, PA: Thomas Publications, 1997

Mysteries of Oak Ridge

1. From Brigadier General Thomas L. Kane to H. Rothermel, attached to a March 21, 1874, letter in the Pennsylvania State Archives, Harrisburg, Pennsylvania.
2. Lt. Francis Wiggin, *Sixteenth Maine Regiment at Gettysburg*; from Bandy, Freeland, Bearss, *The Gettysburg Papers*.
3. David G. Martin, *Gettysburg, July 1*, Conshohocken, PA: Combined Books, 1996.
5. Auditory events are the most common of all paranormal happenings, and many people have reported what sounds like a "cocktail party"—the white noise chattering that is identical to the sounds of a party in the next room. Dorothy Fiedel, author of several ghost books about Lancaster County, Pennsylvania, has confirmed hearing the "party" noise which ceased as she approached. A story about party-like noises in the historic Weikert House appears in *More Ghosts of Gettysburg*, 74-75. And that is exactly the noise one can hear in the background of electronic voice phenomena recordings. It is almost as if the dead were discussing whether they want to talk with us or not.

Be cheerful, sir.
Our revels now are ended. These are our actors,
As I foretold you, were all spirits, and
Are melted into air, into thin air.
—William Shakespeare, *The Tempest*

Mark Nesbitt was born in Lorain, Ohio. He graduated from Baldwin-Wallace College, Berea, Ohio, with a BA in English literature. He worked for the National Park Service as a ranger historian for 5 years and started his own freelance writing and research business in 1977.

Other books by Mark Nesbitt:

Ghosts of Gettysburg

More Ghosts of Gettysburg

Ghosts of Gettysburg III

Ghosts of Gettysburg IV

If the South Won Gettysburg

35 Days to Gettysburg: The Campaign Diaries of Two American Enemies

Rebel Rivers: A Guide to Civil War Sites on the Potomac, Rappahannock, York, and James

Saber and Scapegoat: J.E.B. Stuart and the Gettysburg Controversy

Through Blood and Fire: The Selected Civil War Papers of Maj. Gen. Joshua Chamberlain

Drummer Boy at Gettysburg

Flickertail's Friends.

THOMAS PUBLICATIONS publishes books about the American Colonial era, the Revolutionary War, the Civil War, and other important topics. For a complete list of titles, please visit our web site at:

www.thomaspublications.com

Or write to:

THOMAS PUBLICATIONS
P.O. Box 3031
Gettysburg, PA 17325